# GURU GOBIND SINGH

## (A COLLECTION OF ARTICLES)

**BHUPENDER SINGH**

**RIGI PUBLICATION**



# GURU GOBIND SINGH

(A COLLECTION OF ARTICLES)

BY

BHUPENDER SINGH



Originally published in India

**ISBN: 978-93-91041-43-4**

**Published by RIGI PUBLICATION**

**Printer: Manipal Printers**

777, Street no.9, Krishna Nagar

Khanna-141401 (Punjab), India

Website: www.rigipublication.com

Email: info@rigipublication.com

Phone: +91-9357710014, +91-9465468291

# PREFACE
## (AVANT-PROPOS)

Guru Gobind Singh was a great and remarkable man. But, very little, if anything, is known of his dynamic personality to people other than Sikhs. And, the little that is known is a distorted and confused version of the truth. The Sikhs were fortunate in having at the critical juncture of their history, a devoted leader of vision and courage, who could restate them in terms of the changed environment. And the Khalsa or the Sikh theocracy came into existence. This little book is a collection of fifteen (15) articles covering the biography of the Guru. The endeavour has been to cover all aspects of his life.

The Guru was an extraordinary person; a true patriot, an admirable leader and a brave, fearless and intrepid warrior. He was a social reformer and revolutionary, a democrat and diplomat and above all a saint and a man of God. In addition, he was also a distinguished scholar, a great philosopher, gifted poet, and a polyglot. The Guru was a law giver in the pulpit, a champion in the field, a king in his *masand* (couch or throne) and a *faqir* (ascetic or mendicant) in the society of the Khalsa. He was the right man for the needs of the times.

As a social scientist, Guru Gobind was a trailblazer. He did pioneering work in uplifting the poor and deprived, long before the world woke up to the situation. His motto was: *manas ke jaat sab ek he pahchanbo* – recognize all mankind as one caste. By founding the Khalsa, Guru Gobind erased the caste system and raised the inferiors to the top most level and gave protection to the have-nots and the oppressed; the Khalsa movement saw the rise of the *Dalits* (low castes) and neglected classes/groups. Guru Gobind Singh was the home of the homeless, the honour of the un-honoured, strength of the weak, support of the support-less and the protector of the unprotected.

While staying at Delhi, in May/June 1708, as a token of love for the so called low-castes of Delhi, the Guru shifted to the colony of shoemakers, called Mochi Bagh. The cobblers (*mochis*) served him with utmost devotion. The Guru changed the colony's name to Moti Bagh, the "garden of pearls". Today, a Gurdwara stands at this place on the Ring Road and the colony is still called Moti Bagh.

Guru Gobind Singh was a person with a vision and a dream. Nothing could ruffle or distract him from his chosen path. In everything he wrote or spoke or did there was a note of buoyant hope (*chardi kala*) and the conviction that even if he lost his life, his mission was bound to succeed. There were victories and there were defeats, there were gains and there were losses; but he carried on undeterred till the cruel hands of death snatched him away. Here was a gentleman, who sacrificed all that he had (his parents, four sons, thousands of Sikhs and ultimately himself) for the cause that he espoused. What greater sacrifice can there be?

True, Guru Gobind Singh did not leave his followers a kingdom. He did not succeed in routing the tyrants who held sway over Hindustan, or in liberating the Punjab. But he accomplished much more than that – he liberated the spirit of his people from centuries of apathy and submission and laid the foundation of the Sikh military might by setting up a tradition of reckless valour which became a distinguishing feature of Sikh soldiery.

His courage and faith filled the Punjabis with sanguine hope and confidence which sustained them during the years of persecution after his death. They came to believe in the triumph of their cause as an article of faith, and like their guru asked for no nobler end than death on the battlefield. Guru Gobind Singh left the world, but his mission could not be destroyed; others followed in his footsteps and the fight continued. His legacy lives on.

The traditions set by Guru Gobind Singh have led the Sikhs to attain much name and fame in all spheres of life. It is for the Sikhs to keep up the customs and beliefs that the Guru created for if they are allowed to die, there is little doubt that the Sikh community will die along with them. This is reason enough for a reassessment of the life and teachings of the Guru.

**Note**: In the book there will be repetition of some lines at two or three places. The reason is that the book is a collection of articles written at different times for various purposes and the writings are all interconnected and intertwined.

## ACKNOWLEDGMENTS

I am indebted to Dr Vinita Singh for reading the manuscript, making corrections, and providing valuable suggestions. I can't let this moment pass without acknowledging her immense support and assistance. Her intensity of purpose with incessant enthusiasm and unwavering dedication are praiseworthy. I pass on my personal appreciation for all her timely efforts.

## DEDICATED TO

This book is dedicated to the brave, unknown, and unsung fiery warriors of Guru Gobind Singh, the sentinals and pride of the Sikh nation in making. They laid down their lives fighting the evil and tyrannical forces that were determined to convert the whole country into an Islamic state. It is a tribute to their unrecognized sacrifice, dedication and devotion to their conviction and their Guru. True, they died and many more would die, but not the cause for which they died. Others would come, take their place and the fight would go on till the goal would finally be achieved.

# CONTENTS

# 1

## GURU GOBIND SINGH
### (22 DECEMBER 1666 – 07 OCTOBER 1708)
### (A Tribute and Homage on his Birth Anniversary)

Guru Gobind Rai, the only child and successor of Guru Tegh Bahadur, was born in the early hours of a cold winter morning on 22 December 1666 at Patna. Pir Bhikan Shah came all the way from Punjab to see the newborn child and test his secularism and neutrality towards Muslims and non-Muslims. Gobind became the Guru when he was only nine years old, on 11 November 1675. He was a saint, scholar, poet and warrior and also a polyglot. He had knowledge of Sanskrit and Persian in addition to Hindi and Punjabi and know-how of the Quran. Guru Gobind was a gifted poet and poets sought the Guru's patronage (at one time there were fifty-two poets in his court). He was a versatile genius and in elevating the lowly and downtrodden he did pioneering work long before the birth of Karl Marx and Lenin.

On assessing the situation in the country, Guru Gobind Singh found that a foreign race was ruling the masses and had reduced them to virtual slavery. The state had assumed the form of a purely Islamic nation. There were forced conversions and religious apartheid. In the words of Dr S R Sharma, the Hindus had been reduced to mere "hewers of wood and drawers of water." The Guru's paramount observation was that the people were meek, timid and cowardly and divided among themselves based on caste and creed. On being confronted or in dire straits, they refused their identity and begged their oppressors for mercy. Above all he realised that being truthful, good, right, just, peace loving, humane and principled had no value unless it was backed with power. The verdict of history has always gone in favour of the powerful.

Guru Gobind had a keen insight into human nature and was an adept and admirable leader of men. He contemplated the whole problem and came to the conclusion that nothing could be achieved unless assiduous preparations were made to fight tyranny. He defined his mission as: "to uphold right in every place and destroy sin and evil; that right may triumph, the good may live and tyranny is uprooted from the country." He said, "When all modes of redressing a wrong have failed; raising the sword is just and pious." and "Take the broom of divine knowledge in thy hand and sweep away the filth of timidity." Thus, did he embark on his mission of making the sparrow hunt the hawk; converting the jackal into a lion and making one man fight a legion.

On Baisakhi day (**29 March 1699**) Guru Gobind Singh put his plan into action. He sent *hukamnamas* (edicts or fiats) to his Sikhs and invited them to assemble en masse at Anandpur Sahib for the Baisakhi festival. He addressed the gathering and selected five Sikhs; created the Khalsa with the Five K's and gave the clarion call. The purpose of the formation of the Khalsa and the Five K's had been to choose five men of tested courage and loyalty to constitute the nucleus of the new order, the Khalsa. Guru Gobind Singh was seeking to infuse into a somewhat disorganized band of followers a spirit of unity, courage, and discipline. And, nor can we doubt the tremendous influence which it has exercised in moulding of the Sikh character. Khalsa is an order of 'saint soldiers' dedicated to both piety and justice, and pursuing both with a determination, which when necessity compels, may involve the use of the sword. This is the Khalsa ideal and much that we find in subsequent Sikh history is an obvious response to this ideal.

Guru Gobind's motto was: *manas ke jaat sab ek he pahchanbo* – recognize all mankind as one caste. Thus, the phrase '*Deg Teg Fateh*' (May our caldron i.e., kitchen or charity and our arms be victorious) came in vogue. Charity and wielding of the sword for a just cause hold a special place in the Sikh faith. Charity is the greatest gift that saves life. The Guru said, "He, who serves the poor and needy, serves me. The mouth of the poor and hungry is the Guru's receptacle of gifts - (*Graib da Munh Guru Ki Golakh*)." The sword eradicates oppression and tyranny and establishes righteousness. **These two things contributed the most to the popularity and power of the Sikhs and their church**.

The Sikhs implicitly believed that:

The Khalsa shall rule.
Their enemies (non-believers) will be scattered.
Only they that seek refuge will be saved.

The Khalsa leadership, therefore, came to be comprised mostly of those who from the time of Manu had been denied any respectable status in the *Varna* (caste) based Hindu society and the Khalsa movement became synonymous with the rise of hereto neglected classes/groups/individuals. It was observed that even those people who had been dregs of humanity were changed, as if by magic into something rich and strange. The sweepers, barbers and confectioners who had never touched a sword, and whose ancestors had lived as groveling slaves of the so-called higher classes, became doughty warriors under the stimulating leadership of Guru Gobind Singh. They never shrank from fear and were ready to jump into the jaws of death at the bidding of their Guru.

Guru Gobind did not allow his movement to become anti-Islamic, although his father, the ninth Guru, Tegh Bahadur (1621-1675) had been executed by the order of Aurangzeb in 1675. And, also despite the fact that two of his sons died fighting the Mughals and the remaining two were executed by the orders of the Muslim Governor of Sirhind, he continued to have Muslim friends and attendants. He paid the price for this when he was murdered in October 1708 by two Muslims. When some Sikhs complained against Bhai Kanhaiya for serving water to wounded soldiers, including those belonging to the enemy camp, the Guru patted him on the back and said that it was Kanhaiya who had imbibed the real spirit of Sikhism.

An important trait of the Guru's splendid personality was his sangfroid nature. Nothing could ruffle him. He took the greatest of difficulties in his stride. Among the disastrous misfortunes, setbacks, and circumstances, he stood rock solid and did not lose his equanimity in thought, action, and behavior. In the Sikh religion, a Guru occupies an extremely high and important place, and the Sikhs are intensely loyal to their Gurus. In the times of Guru Gobind Singh this was more so because it was an adverse and tumultuous period. And, Guru Gobind was a military leader of high stature; his predominant personality formed a nucleus around which the Sikhs could rally; his disposition, charisma and dynamism gave the Sikhs integration, cohesion, and a sense of corporate unity. Adversity and a powerful, domineering enemy had instilled complete unity of purpose and it was 'One for All and All for One.'

The *beau ideal* of the Punjabis, Guru Gobind Singh was a handsome man, whose feats as a cavalier, swordsman and archer were enough to endear him to a people who gauged a man by his physical prowess. Stories of his prodigious strength and valour multiplied, and he became a legendary figure in his lifetime. The tips of his arrows were said to be mounted with gold to provide for the family of the foe they transfixed, and he was reputed to be able to send his shafts as far as the eye could see. The Punjabis pictured him leading them to battle on a roan stallion. On one hand fluttered his white hawk; in the other flashed his sabre. Their favourite titles for him were, the rider of the blue horse (*nile ghore da asvar*), the lord of the white hawks (*chitian bajan vala*), and the wearer of plumes (*kalgidhar*). While Gobind's picture was in the minds of the people, his words were on their lips. For the amant, there was the sensuous poetry of the earlier days at Paonta; for the downcast, there was the inspiration and reaffirmation of faith; for the defeated, there was the Epistle of Victory (Zafarnama), breathing defiance in every line; for the crusader, there was the heroic ballads full of martial cadence in their staccato lines with a beat like that of a war drum. Above all, in everything he wrote or spoke, or did there was a note of buoyant hope (*chardi kala*) and the conviction that even if he lost his life, his mission was bound to succeed.

Oh lord these boons of Thee I ask,
Let me never shun a righteous task,
Let me be fearless when I go to battle,
Give me faith that victory will be mine,
Give me power to sing thy praise,
And when comes the time to end my life,
Let me fall in mighty strife.

- Guru Gobind Singh

In the Zafarnama (Epistle of Victory) Guru Gobind describes Aurangzeb as a deceitful fox and an irreligious man whose oaths on the Quran were not to be trusted. He also mentions: "It matters little if a jackal through cunning and treachery succeeds in killing two lion cubs, for the lion himself lives to inflict retribution on you." "I shall strike fire under the hoofs of your horses," he wrote to Aurangzeb, "and I will not let you drink the water of my Punjab." When he learnt of the death of his younger sons and mother, he took the news with stoic calm. "What use is it to put out a few sparks when you raise a mighty flame instead?" he wrote.

Guru Gobind fought sixteen battles (big and small). The biggest debacle/reverse that he faced in his whole military career was in the Battle of Chamkaur (07 December 1705). He was besieged by an overwhelming enemy and the odds, in terms of strength, resources, weapons and ground weighed heavily against him. The Guru lost two of his elder sons (Ajit Singh and Jujhar Singh), three of the *Panj Piare* – Five Beloved Ones (Himmat Singh, Mohkam Singh and Sahib Singh), Pandit Kirpa Ram/Singh (the Kashmiri Brahmin) and thirty-three of his beloved stalwart Sikhs (the names of many famous Sikh warriors are included amongst these), besides the ones mentioned earlier. Only five of the forty Khalsa remained alive. The Guru too would have lost his life in this battle had these five Singhs not ordered him to flee the battleground. Out of these five, two remained behind to continue the struggle. When all seemed lost, a Sikh (Sangat Singh) who resembled the Guru put on his dress and went out to fight. While the enemy was celebrating their kill, the Guru and the three Sikhs made good their escape. Ultimately, only the Guru and three Singhs survived. The three Sikhs included Maan Singh and two of the Five Beloved Ones (Daya Singh and Dharam Singh).

Guru Gobind Singh never ever visited Amritsar and the only writing of his in the Guru Granth is perhaps an addition of two lines to a verse by his father on page 1429. The only change the Guru brought in religion was to expose the other side of the coin. Whereas Nanak had propagated goodness, Guru Gobind condemned evil. One preached the love of one's neighbour, the other the punishment of transgressors. Nanak's God loved His saints; Gobind's God destroyed His enemies. (A History of the Sikhs Vol.1 Page 88 by Khushwant Singh).

By creating the Khalsa, Guru Gobind Singh defied the might of the Mughal Empire. He had to fight against enemies that outsized him in numbers, weapons, equipment, stores, and rations. On the asset side was his superb leadership and the fighting skills and qualities (bravery, loyalty, devotion, determination, perseverance, and sincerity) of his fiery troops. He sacrificed his parents, four sons, thousands of Sikhs and ultimately himself. Here was a man who sacrificed all that he had for the cause that he espoused. What greater sacrifice can there be?

At Nanded, Guru Gobind Singh met **Banda Singh Bahadur** (the famous Sikh general); gave him charge of the military leadership of the Sikhs and asked him to carry forward the mission that he had so assiduously started. He passed away an hour and a half after midnight on 07 October 1708, at the age of 42 after bestowing the Guruship on the Guru Granth Sahib.

True, Guru Gobind Singh did not leave his followers a kingdom; but he laid the foundation of the Sikh military might by setting up a tradition of reckless valour which became a distinguishing feature of Sikh soldiery. They came to believe in the triumph of their cause as an article of faith, and like their guru asked for no nobler end than death on the battlefield.

With clasped hands this boon I crave
When time comes to end my life
Let me fall in mighty strife.

Exactly a hundred years after Guru Gobind Singh's call to arms in 1699, the Sikh Kingdom was founded in 1799 by Maharaja Ranjit Singh.

**References**:


1. The Encyclopedia of Sikhism – Harbans Singh (Editor-in Chief)
2. Sikhism: Glimpses and Glances (Volume 1) – Bhupender Singh
3. History of the Sikhs and their Religion (Volume 1) – Edited by Kirpal Singh and Kharak Singh (published by SGPC)
4. A History of the Sikhs (Volume 1) – Khushwant Singh
5. Guru Gobind Singh – Gopal Singh
6. Homage to Guru Gobind Singh – Khushwant Singh and Suneet Vir Singh
7. The Sikhs and their Scriptures – C H Loehlin
8. Glimpses of The Sikh Gurus (For Children) – Mukhtar S Goraya

# 2

## GENEALOGY OF GURU GOBIND SINGH

With the marriage of Bibi (Lady) Bhani, daughter of Guru Amar Das Bhalla to Guru Ram Das Sodhi, the *Gurugaddi* (seat of Gurus) shifted to the House of Sodhis i.e., from the fourth Guru onwards and became hereditary. Although, fitness rather than primogeniture was always the deciding factor and at time elder sons were overlooked and guruship given to the youngest or even a grandson or a granduncle. But this is the time when all the troubles started in the house of the Sodhi Gurus. Guru Gobind Singh was the only child of Guru Tegh Bahadur and Mata Gujri and he was related to the Gurus of the Sodhi family as follows:

**Guru Tegh Bahadur**, the ninth Guru was the father of Guru Gobind.

**Guru Har Krishan**, the eighth Guru was the son of Guru Har Rai; hence he was the grandnephew of Guru Tegh Bahadur and nephew of Guru Gobind.

**Guru Har Rai**, seventh Guru was the son of Baba Gurditta, the half-brother of Guru Tegh Bahadur. So, he was Guru Tegh Bahadur's nephew and Guru Gobind's cousin.

**Guru Hargobind**, the sixth Guru was Guru Tegh Bahadur's father and Guru Gobind's grandfather.

**Guru Arjan**, the fifth Guru was the father of Guru Hargobind; the grandfather of Guru Tegh Bahadur and the great grandfather of Guru Gobind.

**Guru Ram Das**, the fourth Guru was the father of Guru Arjan, the grandfather of Guru Hargobind, the great grandfather of Guru Tegh Bahadur and thus the great-great grandfather of Guru Gobind.

**Guru Amar Das**, the third Guru was the father of Bibi Bhani (wife of Guru Ram Das); therefore, he was father-in-law of Guru Ram Das and the maternal grandfather of Guru Arjan. Further, he was the maternal great grandfather of Guru Hargobind, the maternal great-great grandfather of Guru Tegh Bhadur, the maternal great-great-great grandfather of Guru Har Rai and Guru Gobind and the maternal great-great-great-great grandfather of Guru Har Krishan.

A lot has been said and written on the Sikh Gurus; there is a plethora of literature available, so there is no need for further elaboration. However, far less is known of most of the women (wives and female relatives) of the Gurus. The Sikh Gurus did a lot for the empowerment of women and their wives came out to meet the Sikh *sangats* (congregations), but the times and social conditions were such (women were considered as property with sexual and reproductive value) that not much emphasis was given to ladies. Moreover, the Sikhs were never good at keeping records and much of their literature was lost or destroyed due to the vagaries of nature and the difficult, turbulent times and circumstances they lived under. Here, we will mostly discuss the distaff side of Guru Gobind Singh's family:

**Mata Mansa Devi** (d. 1569), wife of Guru Amar Das (married on 08 January 1503) and mother of Bibi Dani, Bibi Bhani and two sons Mohan and Mohri, was the daughter of Bhai Dev Chand, a Bahil Khatri of Sankhatra, a small town in Sialkot district (now in Pakistan). Mata Mansa Devi was the mother-in-law of Guru Ram Das, the maternal grandmother of Guru Arjan, the maternal great grandmother of Guru Hargobind, the great-great maternal grandmother of Guru Tegh Bahadur and thus the great-great-great maternal grandmother of Guru Gobind Singh. She died at Goindwal in 1569.

**Bibi Bhani** (b. 1535), was the second of the four children of Guru Amar Das. She had an elder sister Dani (b. 1530) and two younger brothers, Mohri (b. 1539) and Mohan (b. 1536). She was married to Guru Ram Das on 18 February 1554. They had three sons Prithi Chand (b. 1558), Mahadev (b. 1560) and Arjan Dev (b. 1563). She was the great-great grandmother of Guru Gobind Singh. When Emperor Akbar met Guru Amar Das and wanted to make an endowment of land for the Guru ka Langar, an offer which was politely refused by the Guru. It was at Bhai Bhallu's (a barber who embraced the Sikh faith at the hands of Guru Angad and came into prominence at the time of Guru Amar Das) suggestion that the land was gifted to Guru Amar Das's daughter, Bibi Bhani as a wedding present. It was on this site that the holy city of Amritsar came up.

**Mata Ganga Devi** (d. 1621), daughter of Bhai Krishan Chand of village Mau, 10 km west of Phillaur in Punjab, was married to Guru Arjan (1563 – 1606) on 19 June 1589 at her village. She was the mother of Guru Hargobind (born on 19 June 1595 at Vadali, near Amritsar), the grandmother of Guru Tegh Bahadur and the great grandmother of Guru Gobind Singh. She died at Bakala (now Baba Bakala) on 14 May 1621. Her dead body was immersed in River Beas in deference to her wish that her body be consigned to water, as had been her husband's and not cremated (burnt). However, a symbolic cremation was also carried out and a *samadh* (memorial) built at Bakala, which has since been replaced by a shrine named Gurdwara Mata Ganga.

**Mata Nanaki** (d. 1678), the daughter of Hari Chand and Hardel, a well-to-do Khatri couple of Bakala (Amritsar district), was married to Guru Hargobind in April 1613. On 01 April 1621, she became the mother of Guru Tegh Bahadur (the youngest of the five sons of Guru Hargobind). On seeing the newborn child, the Guru predicted that this son of Nanaki would one day be the Guru. Tegh Bahadur grew up into a strong and robust youth and even exhibited military prowess in the battle of Kartarpur (fought by Guru Hargobind against Kale Khan and Painde Khan). But, he was a reserved man, spoke little and remained immersed in meditation and spiritual pursuits.

When Guru Hargobind passed away on 03 March 1644, Mata Nanaki moved to Bakala along with her son and daughter-in-law, Mata Gujri. On 11 August 1664, the prophecy of Guru Hargobind was fulfilled and Tegh Bahadur became Guru. The family moved back to Kiratpur, in the Shivalik foothills where, on 19 June 1665, Guru Tegh Bahadur founded a new habitation and named it after his mother, Chakk Nanaki (now Anandpur). Soon after this Mata Nanaki accompanied her son and daughter-in-law on a long journey to the east. Leaving his mother and wife at Patna, the Guru moved on to Bengal and Assam. At Patna, on 22 December 1666, Mata Nanaki became a grandmother when Guru Gobind Singh was born.

Mata Nanaki lived on for another few years after the execution of her son Guru Tegh Bahadur, on 11 November 1675. It was a great loss, and she was consoled by Mata Gujri and Guru Gobind Singh, her daughter-in-law and grandson. She died in 1678.

**Mata Gujri** (1624 - 1705), was the daughter of Bhai Lal Chand Subhikkhi and Bishan Kaur, a pious couple of Kartarpur (Jalandhar district) and was married to Guru Tegh Bahadur on 04 February 1633. After the marriage ceremony, the newlywed couple came to reside in Amritsar. In 1635, Mata Gujri left Amritsar with her family and went to live at Kiratpur, in the Shivalik foothills. After the death of Guru Hargobind in 1644, she came with her husband and mother-in-law, Mata Nanaki, to Bakala (Amritsar district). Here, they lived in peaceful seclusion with Guru Tegh Bahadur spending his days and nights in meditation and she performing the humble duties of a pious and devoted housewife.

After Tegh Bahadur was installed as Guru in 1664, he started having trouble with his relatives; there were squabbles over the succession to guruship. The Guru was a man of retiring habits and did not fight for his rights and finding no peace, he decided to leave Punjab. Mata Gujri accompanied her husband and mother-in-law on a long journey to the east. The Guru left his family (mother and wife) at Patna and travelled further to Bengal and Assam. It was here, at Patna that Guru Gobind Singh, the only child of Guru Tegh Bahadur and Mata Gujri was born in the early hours of a cold winter morning, on 22 December 1666. She and other members of her family (husband, mother-in-law, and son) were together, once again in March 1671, at Chakk Nanaki (Anandpur).

Mata Gujri showed immense fortitude at the time of parting, when her husband, Guru Tegh Bahadur, left for Delhi on 11 July 1675, prepared to make the supreme sacrifice. Guru Tegh Bahadur was executed on 11 November 1675, and Guru Gobind Singh then being very young, the burden of managing affairs at Anandpur fell on her shoulders. She was assisted in these responsibilities by her younger brother, Kirpal Chand. On the night of 5/6 December 1705, Guru Gobind Singh had to vacate the fort of Anandpur, Mata Gujri and her two grandsons were separated from the main body while they were crossing the rivulet, Sarsa. The three of them were taken by their servant, Gangu, to his village, Kheri, now Saheri (the village was destroyed by Banda Singh Bahadur in 1710, and the habitation that reappeared on its ruins dropped the old name) near Morinda (Ropar district), where he treacherously betrayed them to the local Muslim officer. They were arrested on 08 December and confined to Sirhind Fort in the Thanda Burj (Cold Tower).

On 12 December 1705, the two small grandsons of Mata Gujri, Zorawar Singh and Fateh Singh, aged nine and seven years respectively, were executed and Mata Gujri died of shock. Two kind and august gentlemen, Seth Todar Mall and Moti Ram Mehra conducted their funeral on 13 December 1705. For the cremation, Dewan Todar Mall, bought land by laying out gold coins. This land has been recorded as the costliest land in the world. Moti Ram Mehra sacrificed his whole family just to serve milk to Mata Gujri and her two grandsons, when they were kept hungry for days in severe cold.

At Fatehgarh Sahib, near Sirhind, there is a shrine called Gurdwara Mata Gujri (Thanda Burj). This is where Mata Gujari spent the last four days of her life. About one kilometer to the southeast of it is Gurdwara Joti Sarup, marking the cremation site. Here, on the ground floor, a small domed pavilion in white marble is dedicated to Mata Gujri. Sikhs from far and near come to pay homage to her memory, especially during a three-day fair held from 11- 13 Poh, Bikrami dates corresponding to the last week of December.

**Mata Sulakkhni**, the daughter of Bhai Daya Ram of Anupshahr, in Bulandshahr district of UP, was married to Guru Har Rai in 1640. They had a son, Har Krishan (b. 07 July 1656). Ram Rai (b. 11 March 1646) was her (Mata Sulakkhni's) stepson. Mata Sulakkhni accompanied her son, Guru Har Krishan, when he went to see Emperor Aurangzeb in Delhi. Being the wife of Guru Har Rai, the cousin of Guru Gobind Singh, she was Guru Gobind's sister-in-law.

**Mata Jito**, the daughter of Bhai Hari Jas (a Subhikkhi Khatri of Lahore), was the first wife of Guru Gobind Singh and was married to him on 21 June 1677. Her father had desired that a gala marriage should be performed with pomp and show at Lahore. But the fateful events leading to the martyrdom of Guru Tegh Bahadur intervened. Therefore, a temporary encampment was raised near the village of Basantgarh, 10 km north of Anandpur, and named *Guru ka Lahore* (Guru's Lahore) where the nuptials were held. Mata Jito had three sons – Jujhar Singh (b. 14 March 1691), Zorawar Singh (b. 17 November 1696) and Fateh Singh (b. 25 February 1699). When Guru Gobind Singh was preparing *Khanda da Phul* (stirring water with a double-edged sword or *khanda*) for baptism of Khalsa, Mata Jito appeared with sugar crystals, which were dropped into the iron vessel and sweetness, was thus added to it. Mata Jito died at Anandpur on 05 December 1700 and the cremation took place at Agampura, near Holgarh Fort. A memorial shrine now stands at this site. After her death, her children were looked after by her mother-in-law, Mata Gujari. Some historians are of the view that the Guru had only one wife, Jito, Sundri and Devi were her pet names.

**Mata Sundri** (d. 1747), was the daughter of Bhai Ram Saran, a Kumarav Khatri of Bijvara (Hoshiarpur district of Punjab). She was the second wife of Guru Gobind Singh and was married to him at Anandpur on 04 April 1684. She was the mother of the Guru's eldest son, Ajit Singh (b. 26 January 1687 at Paonta). On the fateful night of 5/6 December 1705, Guru Gobind Singh had to vacate the fort of Anandpur; while crossing the rivulet, Sarsa, the Guru's column was attacked by the enemy. Mata Sundri and Mata Sahib Devan were escorted to Delhi by Bhai Mani Singh. They rejoined the Guru at Talwandi Sabo for sometime during 1706. Here she heard the news of the martyrdom of her son and her stepsons and also of the death of her mother-in-law, Mata Gujri. On this occasion Guru Gobind Singh said, "What difference does it make if four be dead, when thousands are still alive." Mata Sundri went back to stay at Delhi before Guru Gobind set out on his journey to the south, to meet Emperor Aurangzeb.

After the demise of the Guru at Nanded in October 1708, the Sikhs looked up to her for guidance. She appointed Bhai Mani Singh to look after the sacred shrines at Amritsar and also commissioned him to collect the writings of Guru Gobind Singh. She issued *hukamnamas* (edicts) to Sikh *sangats* (congregations), under her own seal and authority. The *hukamnamas* that have since been discovered and published bear dates between 12 October 1717 and 10 August 1730.

Mata Sundri adopted a young boy and named him Ajit Singh (Palit) because of his striking resemblance to her own son (Late Ajit Singh). She had taken over the child from a goldsmith of Delhi; Guru Gobind Singh had warned her that looks could be deceptive. Mata Sundri got him married to a girl from Burhanpur, Tara Bai and he had a son Hathi Singh. Ajit Singh proved to be an ignoble adopted son; he grew arrogant and haughty even towards Mata Sundri; she disowned him and left Delhi and went to live in Mathura with Ajit Singh's wife and son. On 18 December 1725, Ajit Singh was sentenced to death by torture, on the orders of Emperor Muhammad Shah. He was cremated at Sabzi Mandi area, where a shrine was built in his memory. Ajit Singh's son, Hathi Singh was a chip off the old block and followed in the footsteps of his father. He went to live in Burhanpur, where he died issueless. Mata Sundri came back to live in Delhi. She passed away in 1747 and a memorial in her honour stands close to the one commemorating Mata Sahib Devan, in the premises of Gurdwara Bala Sahib (New Delhi).

**Mata Sahib Devan**, the daughter of Bhai Har Bhagwan (aka Ramu) and Jas Devi, a devout Bassi Khatri couple of Rohtas, in Jehlum district (Pakistan). On a visit to Anandpur, in 1700, on the occasion of Baisakhi festival, the couple disclosed to Guru Gobind, their long-cherished desire to give away their daughter in marriage to him. The Guru, who already had two wives and four sons, refused the offer. But when her parents pleaded that their daughter had been brought up as a prospective bride of the Guru and would not countenance marriage with anyone else, he agreed, but made it clear that he would have no physical relations with her. The nuptials took place at Anandpur on 15 April 1700. Her marriage is described as the *kavara dola* (virgin wedlock). Thus, she is known as the virgin wife of Guru Gobind Singh and as an honour the Guru proclaimed her (Mata Sahib Devan) to be the mother of the Khalsa.

On the fateful night of 5-6 December 1705, Guru Gobind Singh had to vacate the fort of Anandpur; while crossing the rivulet, Sarsa, the Guru's column was attacked by the enemy. Mata Sahib Devan and Mata Sundri were escorted to Delhi by Bhai Mani Singh. They rejoined the Guru at Talwandi Sabo for sometime during 1706 and were sent back to Delhi before Guru Gobind Singh set out on his journey to the south, to meet

Emperor Aurangzeb. On learning of the emperor's death, he changed course and went to Agra to meet the new emperor, Bahadur Shah, whom he accompanied to Rajasthan and onward to the Deccan, in 1708. This time, Mata Sahib Devan accompanied him to Nanded, but again shortly before the Guru's assassination in early October 1708, she was persuaded to return to Delhi and stay with Mata Sundri. Mata Sahib Devan, brought five weapons with her from Nanded, that are said to have originally belonged to Guru Hargobind.

From Delhi, Mata Sahib Devan and Mata Sundri, jointly, supervised the affairs of the Sikh community, as is evident from some *hukamnamas* issued in her name to the Sikh *sangats* (congregations) between 1726 and 1734. The exact date of Mata Sahib Devan's death is not known but it is believed that she passed away before Mata Sundri, who died in 1747. The *hukamnamas* issued by her indicate that she must have expired sometime after 1734. The memorial in her honour stands close to the one commemorating Mata Sundri, in the premises of Gurdwara Bala Sahib (New Delhi). The weapons said to have been brought by her from Nanded are preserved as sacred relics in Gurdwara Rikabganj (Parliament Street, New Delhi).

She was the Guru's third wife. Having no children of her own she was honoured by Guru Gobind by being made the mother of the Khalsa. According to Sikh tradition the Guru took her under his protection, but never consummated his relationship with Sahib Devan.

Guru Gobind Singh had four sons. Two elder sons, Ajit Singh (b. 26 January 1687 at Paonta) and Jujhar Singh (b. 14 March 1691) died fighting in the Battle of Chamkaur (07 December 1605). The two younger sons, Zorawar Singh (b. 17 November 1696) and Fateh Singh (b. 25 February 1699) were executed on orders of Wazir Khan, the governor of Sirhind. The fate of Ajit Singh Palit, the adopted son of Mata Sundri is given above.

Another boy, Zorawar Singh Palit (d. 1708), generally known as Guru Gobind Singh's adopted son, was the son of a carpenter, Bhai Natthu of Bassi Pathanan (near Sirhind) and his mother, Mai Bhikkhi, served in the Guru's household at Anandpur. He was about the same age as the Guru's third son Zorawar Singh and both of them were playmates. Once he defeated the *sahibzada* (Guru's son) in a friendly wrestling bout in the presence of the Guru. Guru Gobind Singh lovingly remarked, "He, too, is my Zorawar (literally, strong or mighty son)." And he treated him as such. After vacating Anandpur on the night of 5-6 December 1705, Zorawar Singh Palit managed to cross the flooded Sarsa, but was severely wounded in a skirmish. In another, unexpected skirmish with local soldiers, near Chittorgarh Fort, he died fighting, along with 19 other Sikh soldiers, on 03 April 1708. Shrines commemorating Zorawar Singh Palit exist at Kotla Nihang Khan, Dadheri, Ugani and Khizarabad.

Finally, to summarize and for ease of assimilation, it will be worthwhile to list the names of the family of Guru Gobind Singh in a correct perspective. The list follows:

Mata Jito, Mata Sundri and Mata Sahib Devan – the three wives of Guru Gobind Singh
Ajit Singh (son of Mata Sundri), Jujhar Singh, Zorawar Singh and Fateh Singh (three sons of Mata Jito) – four sons of Guru Gobind Singh
Ajit Singh Palit (adopted son of Mata Sundri) and Zorawar Singh Palit (treated like a son in all respects by Guru Gobind Singh) – the two adopted sons
Guru Tegh Bahadur and Mata Gujri – parents of Guru Gobind Singh
Guru Har Gobind and Mata Nanaki – grandparents of Guru Gobind Singh
Guru Arjan and Mata Ganga Devi – great grandparents of Guru Gobind Singh
Guru Ram Das and Bibi Bhani – great-great grandparents of Guru Gobind Singh and Baba Hari Das (d. 1541) and Anup Devi (Daya Kaur), the **parents of Guru Ram Das**, were the great-great-great grandparents of Guru Gobind
Guru Amar Das and Mansa Devi were the great-great-great maternal grandparents of Guru Gobind Singh and Tej Bhan and Mata Bakht Kaur (aka Lachhammi, Bhup Kaur and Rup Kaur), the **parents of Guru Amar Das**, were the great-great-great-great maternal grandparents of Guru Gobind

Guru Har Rai and Bibi Sulakkhani – Guru Gobind's cousin and sister-in-law
Guru Har KrIshan – son of Guru Har Rai, the cousin of Guru Gobind and hence Guru Gobind Singh's nephew

**Note**: the names and dates given in different books are in variance with each other. It is high time that Sikh scholars and intellectuals put their heads together and came to a consensus.

**References:**


1. The Encyclopedia of Sikhism – Harbans Singh (Editor-in Chief)
2. Sikhism: Glimpses and Glances (Volume 1) – Bhupender Singh
3. History of the Sikhs and their Religion (Volume 1) – Edited by Kirpal Singh and Kharak Singh (published by SGPC)
4. A History of the Sikhs (Volume 1) – Khushwant Singh

# 3

## TRANSFORMATION OF SIKHISM

### Evolution of Khalsa

### (CIRCUMSTANCES, EVENTS, EXPERIENCES AND REASONS)

Guru Gobind Singh, the tenth Guru of the Sikhs was one of the most remarkable men of all times. He was a versatile genius, a saint, scholar, poet, warrior and also a polyglot. An important trait of the Guru's splendid personality was his equipoise. Nothing could ruffle him even in the most difficult of times. He was bold, full of self-assurance and defiant against injustice and evil. And, in elevating the lowly and downtrodden he did pioneering work long before the birth of Karl Marx and Lenin.

Why did Guru Gobind Singh have to form the Khalsa? For an answer to this, you must turn the hands of the clock to the mid-seventeenth century, and that is where the story really begins ....

On studying the prevailing environment, Guru Gobind Singh found that Muslim invaders held sway over the whole country. A foreign race was ruling the masses and had reduced them to virtual slavery. They were holding the nation to ransom and oppression, suppression, repression, and exploitation of the common people was rampant in the state. The worst was that tyranny and humiliation of the repressed masses had crossed all limits and the state had assumed the form of a purely Islamic nation. There were forced conversions and religious apartheid. The minority ruled the majority, who were helpless and at their mercy.

The plight of the masses was miserable. The condition of women was deplorable. Might was right and tyranny and persecutions were justified. Centuries of social and political discrimination had made the people feel hapless. Chaos, anarchy, and lack of leadership had deprived the people of the will to resist. There was human catastrophe and the land was littered with crime and human rights violations, with attempts to change the fabric of the country and make it an absolute Muslim state.

The public was conspicuous in their silence and absence. They were cowards and full of fear. The land was covered with a blanket of silence. There had been silence for so long, over the centuries that the natives had lost the desire to revolt; to fight back and to raise their voice against the wrongs and atrocities committed on them. They had their identity, dignity, reputation, religion, culture, language, families, and everything to lose but they still kept quiet. They were custodians of the inheritance of future generations, who would ask them what they were doing when their inheritance was being squandered away; history would ask for accountability.

The religion of this alien, reigning clan was Islam. The real issues that agitated the minds of the people were intense divisions within society, forced conversions to Islam, and unending oppression and suffering. Non-Muslims were singled out for discriminatory treatment. Most important jobs and posts were reserved for Muslims, *Jazia* (a religious tax) was imposed on non-Muslims and they were forbidden to build or repair their temples and the existing religious places were being razed to the ground.

Many of the followers of Vishnu, Shiva, and the other gods of the Hindu dispensation adopted during that period the faith of the Arabian prophet, as the result of force or with a view to worldly advantage. Due to forced, rampant conversions and religious segregation, more than half of the population had already been converted to Islam and at this rate the day was not far when the whole of north India would turn Muslim. On refusing to change their faith, Guru Gobind Singh's great grandfather, Guru Arjan, was mercilessly tortured to death on the banks of the River Ravi, his grandfather, Guru Hargobind was captured and incarcerated in Gwalior Fort, in Madhya Pradesh and his father, Guru Tegh Bahadur, was beheaded in Chandni Chowk, Delhi.

When Guru Tegh Bahadur's beheaded body lay in Chandni Chowk, nobody from the high caste Sikhs came forward to claim the remains of their Guru for cremation. When questioned by the officials whether they were Sikhs, they had the fear and weakness to deny their religion. Guru

Gobind saw in this the danger of a backsliding among the Sikhs. He vowed, therefore, that he would make it impossible for the Sikhs to hide their creed in future; that he would give them such distinguishing marks that even one of them among millions would stand out from a distance and be easily recognized.

The Guru's cardinal finding was that the people were meek, timid, and cowardly and divided among themselves based on caste and creed. On being encountered or in dire straits, they refused their identity and begged their persecutors for mercy. He felt sad on seeing the pathetic plight of the people. Guru Gobind was a visionary with a keen insight into human nature and was imbued with qualities of a leader. He deliberated on the problem and came to the conclusion that nothing could be achieved unless diligent and concerted preparations were made to fight tyranny.

It dawned on Guru Gobind that being good, truthful, peace-loving, and principled had no value unless it was backed with power. History had proved this, time and time again. The verdict of history has always gone in favour of the powerful. The famous quote of Mao Tse Tung, "*Power grows out of the barrel of a gun*," amply justifies this. If you want peace you have to be prepared for war. The Guru realised that time had come for them to pick up arms and fight.

The people had to stand up to face the oppressor, they had to rise to guard their inheritance and they had to fight for their self-respect and sovereignty. The Guru's task was to unite the people, divided among themselves based on caste and creed and to rejuvenate and revitalize the population. Guru Gobind was a far-sighted man and was looking into the future. It was now for him to arouse and raise the spirits of the meek and timid Hindus and forge a casteless militant fraternity that could fight for its rights. He had to motivate those, who refused to fight back and begged their oppressors for mercy and to change their attitude. This timidity had to be shed and hence forth the tide reversed. According to G C Narang, '*The object that the Guru (Gobind Singh) set before himself was to infuse a new life in the dead bones of Hindus to make them forget their differences and present a united front against the tyranny and persecution to which they were exported.*'

The tyranny of the Turks had certainly become intolerable. Guru Gobind Singh realized that the people should wear arms and be always ready to defend themselves. He preached to his people the advantages of being armed and physically fit. They who practiced the use of weapons should develop their martial instincts, enhance their prestige, and defend their property, while those who remained in the slough of ancient apathy would lose all that they possessed. The Sikhs could be maintained as a nation only by bravery and skill in weapons. They were enjoined to practice arms and not show their backs to the foe in battle. They were ever to help the poor and protect those who sought their security and shelter (refuge). "As I have raised you from a lowly to a lofty position by imparting to you spiritual knowledge, so must you now rise by your skill in arms and bravery and fight for your dignity, self-respect and sovereignty," said Guru Gobind Singh.

Another serious problem confronting the Guru was that the Sikh community faced the twin dangers of relapsing into Hinduism and annihilation by fanatical Islam which was in ascendance in the Mughal court. Before the inception of the Khalsa the Sikhs of Brahmin and Kshatriya origin were most influential members of the community. Idolatry, washing sins in sacred rivers, caste marks, caste distinctions, wearing the sacred thread, rituals and superstitions were a common practice among Sikhs. Guru Gobind Singh wanted to retain the plebeian (ordinary people) and unadulterated character of the movement started by Baba Nanak. He inferred that education was mandatory to eradicate ignorance for a man without learning could not distinguish between right and wrong. The Guru requested the Brahman pundits (Sikhs and others) who had taken residence in his *durbar* to teach Sikhs the Sanskrit language. They refused saying that Sanskrit was *deva bhasa* (language of the gods) and could not be taught to *Sudras* (low castes).

Many historians feel that there were four pertinent considerations for the creation of the Khalsa by Guru Gobind Singh:

- The first and foremost was the atrocities of the Mughals (especially Aurangzeb) and Muslims.
- The second was the internal condition of Sikhism that was not healthy, and forces of disintegration were at work within the religion. The *Masand* system had become totally corrupt. The *masands*, from the Persian word masnad (couch), were agents or tax/offering collectors for the Gurus. Disunity and decadence had crept into the movement launched by Guru Nanak and there were squabbles over the succession to guruship. After the fourth Guru, Ram Das, guruship had come into the house of the Sodhi Gurus and become hereditary and the relatives of the Gurus (Prithi Chand - the elder brother of Guru Hargobind, and his son Mehrban, Dhir Mal – the brother of Guru Har Rai, and Ram Rai – the elder brother of Guru Harkrishan) vied and quarreled for the guruship. This was leading to factionalism and schism among Sikhs.
- The third was the caste system which was a stumbling block in the way of unity and brotherhood among the Hindus.
- Lastly there were many Jats among the Sikhs who were brave and loved adventure and warfare. They preferred the sword to the rosary. The creation of the Khalsa would be in consonance with their taste and nature. They had to be kept within the fold, for the chosen path to be followed. Henceforth they were needed for the military operations and turbulent times that were imminent (this has been questioned by some scholars and they are not totally in accord with this reason).

On a close scrutiny, it will be found that **the main aim of this entire exercise of Guru Gobind Singh to form the Khalsa was to obliterate all distinctions of caste, creed and religion and to follow one creed and one path**. Once caste was annihilated, the other aims would automatically take care of themselves. Guru Gobind's motto was: *manas ke jaat sab ek he pahchanbo* – recognize all mankind as one caste.

Guru Gobind Singh was determined to seek justice for the murder of his father and the atrocities of the Mughals and also save the honour of his country. The challenge of the Mughal Empire was the turning point in the history of the Sikhs. The Sixth Guru Hargobind was the first to appeal to arms; the Tenth (Guru Gobind Singh) had to put the army on a regular footing. Guru Gobind Singh and his followers had to fight these brutal forces single handedly.

The problems had to be solved and the ground prepared before any definite steps towards reformation could be affected. The final confrontation between the right to live in peace in one's own faith and the proselytizing intolerance of the crusading-conqueror rulers had to come sooner or later and the people had to be ready for it. The Khalsa was intended to be a body of dedicated people who were pledged to ensure the victory of dharma (truth) over evil. The Khalsa was to be an order best contended by serving others for the good of all. It must be emphasized that as planned and visualized by the Guru, while the Khalsa was expected to acquire the skills of a soldier, he was permitted to use his sword only for a noble cause, to resist oppression and tyranny, and to secure justice and equality for humanity. **As a matter of fact, the formation of Khalsa grew out of the necessity of suppressing the oppressors.**

Guru Nanak's teachings became an instrument of social change and gave roots to a socio-religious movement, and it led to political developments that turned the course of history. It created an awakening that had an impact beyond the times of Nanak, into the future. It enabled Guru Gobind Singh nearly a century and a half later in 1699, to transform an oppressed and helpless people to the leonine (resembling loins) men of the Khalsa. The work initiated by Nanak was completed by Gobind. G C Narang has rightly stated, *"The seed that blossomed in the time of Guru Gobind Singh had been sown by Guru Nanak and watered by his successors. The sword which earned the Khalsa's way to glory was undoubtedly forged by Gobind, but the steel was provided by Nanak."*

It was only after duly considering the given times and conditions, earnestly debating the prevailing situation, profound rumination, and serious deliberation that Guru Gobind decided to form the Khalsa (a brotherhood of saint-soldiers). These saint-soldiers were to be ever prepared to fight for the cause of justice, in defense of the poor, the oppressed and the downtrodden. Guru Gobind Singh had charted a massive programme of rejuvenating and reshaping the society. He wanted to give a distinct appearance to the Sikhs so that they would be recognized from a distance, and it would be impossible for them to hide their identity. Guru Gobind Singh defined his mission as: "to uphold right in every place and destroy sin and evil; that right may triumph, the good may live and tyranny is uprooted from the country." He said, "When all modes of redressing a wrong have failed; raising the sword is just and pious." and "Take the broom of divine knowledge in thy hand and sweep away the filth of timidity." Thus, did he embark on his mission of making the sparrow hunt the hawk; converting the jackal into a lion and making one man fight a legion.

On Baisakhi day (**29 March 1699**) he put his plan into action; founded the Khalsa and gave the clarion call. The purpose of the formation of the Khalsa and the Five K's was first and foremost to end the caste system and unite the people. Gobind Singh was seeking to inject into a somewhat disorganized band of followers a spirit of unity, courage, and discipline. The birth of the Khalsa marked the culmination of the evolution of the Sikh movement. Thus, did Guru Gobind Singh transform his followers from the pacifist Sikh into the militant Khalsa. **From now on the weapons would speak**.

**References:**

1. The Encyclopedia of Sikhism (Volume 2) – Harbans Singh (Editor-in Chief)
2. Sikhism: Glimpses and Glances (Volume 1) – Bhupender Singh
3. History of the Sikhs and their Religion (Volume 1) – Edited by Kirpal Singh and Kharak Singh (published by SGPC)
4. A Short History of The Sikhs (Volume 1) – Teja Singh and Ganda Singh
5. A History of the Sikhs (Volume 1) – Khushwant Singh
6. Sikhism (Its Philosophy and History) - Edited by Daljeet Singh and Kharak Singh (published by Institute of Sikh Studies)

# 4

## THE KHALSA AND THE FIVE Ks
### (FROM THE TRANQUIL SIKH TO THE BELLICOSE KHALSA)

On Baisakhi day (**29 March 1699**) Guru Gobind Singh decided to give practical shape to his ideas and he put his project into force. He invited the Sikhs to assemble en masse at Anandpur Sahib for the Baisakhi festival. He addressed the gathering and selected five Sikhs. They were **Daya Ram** a Khatri from Lahore, **Dharam Das** a Jat from Hastinapur (Meerut-UP), **Himmat Rai** a water carrier from Jagan-nath Puri, **Mohkam Chand** a *cheemba* (calico printer) from Dwarka and **Sahib Chand** a barber from Bidar. They, the *Panj Payare* (five beloved ones) were all in their thirties and came from different Hindu castes (four of them being from lower and depressed classes) and hailed from far off places as Bidar (Karnataka), Puri (Orissa) and Dwarka (Gujarat).

The Guru baptized the five by making them drink *Amrit* (nectar of immortality), prepared by a *khanda* (double edged sword) from the same bowl. They were thus initiated into the casteless fighting fraternity which he named the **Khalsa** (the chosen ones). The Khalsa was called the "Army of the Supreme Ruler of the Universe" (*Akal Purakh Kee Fauj*) and based on the cardinal principles (named after the five beloved ones) of Daya (compassion), Dharam (righteousness), Himmat (courage), Mokham (determination), and Sahib (master) which the Khalsa was to follow scrupulously in war and peace. Thus, did Guru Gobind Singh transform his followers from the pacifist Sikh into the militant Khalsa.

Before their initiation into the new community, the *panj payare* took an oath renouncing their previous occupations (*kirt nash*) for that of soldering; their family ties (*kul nash*) to become the family of Gobind (Khalsa fraternity); their earlier creeds (*dharma nash* - there were different rules for each caste) for the creed of the Khalsa; and rituals (*karm nash*) except that sanctioned by the Sikh faith.

They were also to observe the four *rahats* or rules of conduct: not to cut their hair; not to eat *halal* (animal slaughtered in the Muslim fashion) meat; not to smoke, chew tobacco or consume alcoholic beverages and lastly not to violate the modesty of any woman (even the enemy's). Retaliation against women was banned.

They were made to take an oath to observe the Five Ks, namely hair (*Kesh*); comb (*Kangha*); steel bangle (*Kara*) on the right wrist; sword (*Kirpan*) and knee long drawers (*Kachchh*).

The initiated ones were enjoined to suffix '*Singh*' or lion (current among Hindu martial classes) and all women '*Kaur*' or lioness/princess to their names instead of their surnames (it gives a person's caste), which meant that all baptized Sikhs belonged to one family. The common name identifies each person as a part of the community, as part of the same family, and as willing to fight for the faith.

If we analyse and dissect the above principles of the Khalsa it will be found that the main aim of the entire exercise was to obliterate all distinctions of caste, creed, and religion and to follow one creed and one path. The other aims would automatically take care of themselves. The Guru had realized that the only remedy to all the ills that plagued the Sikh society was the creation of the Khalsa and **the main purpose of creating the Khalsa was to do away with the caste system that was the downright and root cause of all evil and a stumbling block in the way of unity and brotherhood among the Hindus**. Once this was done all other goals would fall in place, on their own.

The Khalsa was to adopt the way of cooperation, mix freely with one another and no one was to deem himself superior to another. They were to receive baptism, eat out of the same vessel, and feel no disgust or contempt for one another. Guru Gobind's motto was: *manas ke jaat sab ek he pahchanbo* – recognize all mankind as one caste. Making people drink *amrit* out of a common bowl (the orthodox Hindu practice considered food or drink touched by a lower caste as polluted) was to break through the orthodox caste system. Similarly giving the name

'*Singh*' to all men and '*Kaur*' to all women instead of their surnames was a step in the same direction.

After baptizing the five, Guru Gobind Singh was in turn baptized by them. The poet subsequently sang, "*Wah Wah!* Guru Gobind Singh *Appe Gur-Chela*." (Guru Gobind Singh was hailed as himself being Master as well as disciple). He was no longer their superior but had merged his entity in the Khalsa. At the end of the ceremony, they hailed each other with the new greeting – *Wahe Guru Ji ka Khalsa – Wahe Guru Ji ke Fateh* – The Khalsa is the chosen of God – Victory is to God. On the first day about twenty thousand men came into the fold and according to one estimate as many as eighty thousand (80,000) Sikhs were initiated in a few days. It was now left to Guru Gobind Singh to teach the Khalsa the use of arms as well as to convince them of the morality of employment of force.

The creation of the Khalsa saw the rise of the downtrodden and gave protection to the deprived and the oppressed. The Sikhs got a new and separate identity and there was significant increase in their numbers. A new spirit of sacrifice, patriotism and bravery was instilled in the Sikhs which led to successful opposition of the tyrannical Mughal rule.

With its inception, Sikhism had done away with caste and the institution of *Langar* and *Sewa* were deeply embedded, however it was for Guru Gobind Singh to further strengthen and amalgamate them. Thus, the phrase '*Deg Teg Fateh*' came in vogue. *Deg* means a cauldron/kettle/kitchen - to feed the poor and needy. *Teg* means a sword - a symbol of freedom and sovereignty and the protector of the weak and helpless. And, *Fateh* means victory. Hence, it means **'Prosperity in Peace and Victory in War'** or in other words it literally means **'May our charity and our arms be victorious.'** Charity and wielding of the sword for a just cause hold a special place in the Sikh Faith. Charity is the greatest gift that saves life. The Guru said, "He, who serves the poor and needy, serves me. The mouth of the poor and hungry is the Guru's receptacle of gifts - (*Graib da Munh Guru Ki Golakh*)." The Sword eradicates oppression and tyranny and establishes righteousness. **These**

**two things contributed the most to the popularity and power of the Sikhs and their church.**

Ideologically, the Khalsa aimed at a balanced combination of the ideals of *bhakti* and *shakti*, or to express in modern terminology: the Khalsa was to be a brotherhood in faith and a brotherhood in arms at one and the same time. All this was an absolute must to forge a sect of pacifists into a militant brotherhood of crusaders – 'saint-soldiers' (*sant-sepahi*). It was mandatory for the unity and solidarity of the Khalsa fraternity. It was a historical need - a predominant and urgent demand of the prevailing times.

The Sikhs implicitly believed that:

The Khalsa shall rule.
Their enemies (non-believers) will be scattered.
Only they that seek refuge will be saved.

The Khalsa was meant to be a saint (*sant*) and a soldier (*sepahi*). Now a question may arise: What was the need of saint soldiers? In the days before Guru Nanak there was duality in all religious traditions between spiritual and empirical (based on observation or experience) needs. Worldly activities were considered incompatible and a hinderance to spiritual progress. So for spiritual men the selfish components of renunciation, asceticism, celibacy, and ahimsa (non-violence) were essential (altruism was utterly lacking) and this made them parasites on society. In the caste system all aspects of social behaviour of each sub-caste were regulated by fixed rules and codes. The rigid rules had religious sanction of the Vedas and were confirmed by the *avtars* (manifestation of a diety in bodily form on earth) of Vishnu, incarnated as Lord Rama and Krishna.

Lord Rama known as *Maryada Purshotam* (best man who practiced propriety) is said to have cut off the head of a Sudra (low caste untouchable) for the sole crime of indulging in religious rites not allowed by his caste. Lord Krishna was supposed to have asserted that he was the creator of *Chaturvarna* (four castes). The unchangeable or unadaptable enforcement of caste system and negative religious beliefs ensured internal social stability and control of the crafty and shrewd Brahmins for nearly three thousand years. The Sudras and all women were deprived of the right to education. When knowledge lies in the hands of a few there is bound to be exploitation. But, such an unjust system taking undue advantage of people could not last forever. Jainism and Buddhism rose as protest movements against Brahmanical ritualism and superstition. At the birth of Christ and for seven hundred years or more, the predominant faith of India was Buddhism. Buddhist texts state that the Brahmin Pusphyamitra Shunga persecuted the Buddhist monks and overthrew the Buddhist Maurya Empire. Gradually the astute and cunning Brahmins were once again able to restore Hinduism.

Majority of the population had been disarmed and the shabby, mean, and cruel treatment of the Shudras and even the Vaishyas (working classes) did not win the higher castes their confidence, friendship, sympathy or loyality. The consequence was that when the Muslim conquests of India began they met with no formidable resistance. Therefore, Guru Gobind Singh, rather than laying emphasis on a single quality created a balanced and holistic society with full development of individuals, covering every aspect of their life, physical, temporal, moral, and spiritual. This saw the birth of the Khalsa or saints as well as soldiers and not saints or soldiers. The first and the largest members of this new community were the humble and lowly people who had suffered for centuries under the draconian *Varna* dharma and the tyrannical rule of the foreign invaders.

Before proceeding further, it would be worthwhile to explore the meaning of the word Khalsa. Khalsa is an Arabic word. It stands for the land that belongs to the king and not to an individual. It means **crownlands** administered directly by the king or lands directly under government management. Till some time back this word was commonly used in maintaining revenue records in Indian languages. The 6th and 9th Gurus have addressed the Sikh *sangat* (commonwealth) as Khalsa in their *hukamnamahs* (epistles). The word occurs once in the Sikh scriptures. The word Khalsa is used there for the fearless worshippers of

God almighty. On page 655 of the Guru Granth Sahib, Bhagat Sheikh Kabir in his couplet says,

"*Those slaves of God who love to worship Him have become Khalsa.*"
*Kaho Kabir jan bhaiye Khalse prem bhagat jih jaani*

Khalsa is a Persio-Turkish administrative term, which means royal, not subordinate to anyone, answerable to none subordinate, sovereign, directly administered by the Sovereign. To interpret the meaning of Khalsa as pure may create a wedge between the Khalsa and other non-Khalsa people. Therefore, the literal meaning of the word Khalsa (the chosen ones) would be sovereign (though both meanings – pure/clean and sovereign are prevalent).

The creation of the new order (Khalsa) had manifold ramifications. It caused a great stir, while some embraced the order of the Khalsa readily, others were reluctant. They found the code too tough and incompatible with family traditions and customs. The situation led to dissensions among Sikhs and tension between Sikhs and non-Sikhs. The higher castes by and large remained aloof. Some of them professed that they had faith in the religion of Sri Guru Nanak Dev and other Gurus but refused to adopt the Five Ks and change to the new order. Those who did not accept the changes brought about by Guru Gobind Singh began thereafter to be addressed as *Sahaj Dhari* (those who take time to change or those who take it easy or slow adopters) Sikhs as opposed to the *Singh/Kesh Dhari/Amrit Dhari/Khalsa* Sikhs. Later the British called them the Sikhs of Nanak and the Sikhs of Gobind. **Thus, not all Sikhs belong to the Khalsa order**.

The Khalsa leadership, therefore, came to be comprised mostly of those who from the time of Manu had been denied any respectable status in the *Varna* based Hindu society. Since the Khalsa order repudiated caste and other distinctions based on wealth, profession, culture, creed, etc. Jats and other socially neglected classes rejoiced, and the Khalsa movement became synonymous with the rise of hereto neglected classes or groups/individuals. It was observed that even those people who had been dregs of humanity were changed, as if by magic into something rich and strange. The sweepers, barbers and confectioners who had never touched a sword, and whose ancestors had lived as groveling slaves of the so-called higher classes, became doughty warriors under the stimulating leadership of Guru Gobind Singh. They never shrank from fear and were ready to jump into the jaws of death at the bidding of the Guru.

The prospects of improved status which Islam offered to the lower sections of the Hindu society were now available from Sikhism as well because Sikhism, too, like Islam, made no distinction between the high and low. In so far as Sikhism was closer to the roots of Hindu culture, for the Hindu masses it had an edge over Islam. Therefore, for those who wanted to change their religion with a view to improving their position in society preferred Sikhism to Islam. And some of the Musalmans, generally former converts from Hinduism, began to show more interest in Sikhism than in Islam.

The character and development of the Sikh movement had three main social goals: (a) create an egalitarian society (b) use the new society as a base to wage an armed struggle against religious and political oppression and (c) seize political power for the Khalsa. These aims were an integral part of Sikh thesis and ethos that injustice, inequality, and hierarchism, in whatsoever form must be always combated everywhere and every time.

Nowhere has Guru Gobind Singh given the how and why of the significance of the Five Ks. Perhaps after the baptism ceremony, the turbulent period that followed did not give him much time. But they are not very difficult to understand. The Five Ks are a set of five distinctive features or elements of personal appearance or apparel that set the Sikhs apart (give a separate identity) from the followers of any other religious faith. Since they all start with the letter K, hence the name Five Ks.

***Kesh*** or unshorn hair imprints on the individual, the investiture of the spiritual man exemplified in Hinduism by *rishis* or sages and even of God Himself (whose epithet *keshava* means one who carries long tresses). *Kesh* also signify strength (Samson in the Bible), manliness, virility, courage and dignity, and therefore signify qualities both of a *sant* (saint) and a *sipahi* (soldier) and a life both of *bhakti* (spiritual devotion) and *shakti,* i.e. strength of conviction, of courage, and of fortitude. Keeping the times and conditions in view, it was more convenient and made a man look brave, fierce and intimidating on the battlefield. Sometimes long scientific explanations of the advantages of full-grown hair are furnished, which are really needless. It is enough to say that the Sikhs keep their hair untrimmed and uncut because it is one of their **religious vows** and a clear mark of **identification**. The other four emblems are complimentary to this one and the profession of soldering.

***Kangha*** (the small comb required to keep the hair tidy) symbolizes cleanliness. As a vestured symbol, it appears to **repudiate** the practice of keeping the hair matted. The *kangha* is a small wooden comb stuck in the chignon on top of the head and the turban tied over it. Thus, it becomes a part and parcel of the body and is carried on the hair at all times. Hence it is handy whenever and wherever time permitted its use and requirement, in that stormy age.

***Kirpan*** (the sword) signifies valour. For Guru Gobind Singh the sword was the emblem of divine energy for the destruction of the evil and protection of the good. It is also called *bhagauti* (*bhagvati* or the goddess Durga, slayer of the demons) which in Sikh vocabulary stands for the sword as well as for the Almighty. The sword is considered synonymous with God. The sword is also a symbol of freedom and sovereignty. Unlike a dagger, which is a weapon of clandestine attack, the sword is a weapon of open combat. The *kirpan* is a symbol of active resistance against evil. The word *kirpan* seems to have been compounded from ***kirpa*** (compassion) and ***an*** (honour, dignity). Hence as a symbolic weapon it shall only be wielded in compassion (to protect the oppressed) and for upholding righteousness and human dignity. It stands therefore, for the heroic affirmation of honour and valour for the vindication of ethical principles. In praise of the sword Guru Gobind Singh says:

> "Sword, that smiteth in a flash,
> That scatters the armies of the wicked
> In the great battlefield;
> O thou symbol of the brave,

Thine arm is irresistible, thy brightness shineth forth
Thy blaze and splendour dazzling like the sun.
Sword thou-art the protector of the saints,
Thou art the scourge of the wicked;
Scatterer of sinners; I take refuge in thee
Hail to the Creator, Saviour and Sustainer,
Hail Thee: Sword Supreme."

***Kara*** (the steel bangle) was adopted as a pragmatic accessory to the *kirpan.* A set of strong steel bangles used to be worn by warriors as protective armour over the arm that wielded the sword. But besides the pragmatic self-defense value, it has a deeper symbolic significance. As a circle it signifies perfection, without beginning, without end. Traditionally, a circle also represents dharma, the Supreme Law, and Divine Justice. It also symbolizes restraint and control. The *Kara,* therefore, symbolizes for the Sikhs a just and lawful life of self-discipline (*rahit*) and self-control (*sanjam*).

***Kachchh*** (pair of long shorts) As a pragmatic explanation, its sartorial design makes for greater agility and easy movements, thereby ensuring ready preparedness, *tayyar bar tayyar*, (readiness beyond ordinary readiness). This garment the *Kachchh* was adaptable to the horse (i.e. it also served as a horseman's riding breeches) and its design made for quick and easy movement while running and fighting (on foot or on horseback). It was a fighting man's uniform of those times. As a symbol it also signifies manly control.

The virtues that each of the Five Ks indicated were: *Kesh* for saintliness, *Kangha* for cleanliness, *Kirpan* to fight for *dharma* (righteousness), *Kachchh* for chastity and *Kara* for determination.

In those tumultuous times the Sikhs lived in jungles as outlaws. The Mughal governors were part of an evil and brutal regime and butchers of the Khalsa. The Sikhs were hunted, and a price lay on their heads. Their only fault being that they were Sikhs. This persecution lasted for well over a century and a half (from the early seventeenth century to three quarters of the eighteenth century). In these trying times, the Khalsa carried only light articles and weapons that were handy and ready for use and could be carried on horse or foot. Therefore, the five Ks formed a part and parcel of the body of a Khalsa; he ate, slept, and moved with them always - every time and everywhere. This was an added asset for it made the Khalsa ever ready for action, weather it was to fight, flee or protect when surprised. The Five Ks enabled the Khalsa to be ready at a moment's notice in case of sudden need. The greatest advantage was that the Khalsa being forever prepared, light equipped, and self-contained was thus unencumbered and always ready to act. He could not afford the luxury of hesitation for delay spelled disaster.

The Five Ks made the Khalsa conspicuous and easily identifiable. They stood out from a distance and had no means to deny their identity. It is also likely that, by making his followers easily recognizable by virtue of their turbans and beards, the Guru wanted to raise a body of men who would not be able to deny their faith when in danger but whose external appearance would invite persecution and in turn breed courage to resist it. When besieged, they knew that the enemy would give them no quarter, so they had to either fight to the finish or emerge victorious. Capture would mean a disgraceful and ignoble change of faith or a brutal and cruel death. With the end result vividly evident to them, the choice lay between victory and death (Do or Die). This was the greatest quality that made them fearless and ferocious fighters.

Sun Tzu in his book *The Art of War* says, "Soldiers when in desperate straits lose the sense of fear. If there is no place for refuge, they will stand firm." And again, "Throw your soldiers into positions whence there is no escape, and they will prefer death to flight, officers and men alike will put forth their uttermost strength."

The purpose of the formation of the Khalsa and the Five K's had been to choose five men of tested courage and loyalty to constitute the nucleus of the new order, the Khalsa. Guru Gobind Singh was seeking to infuse into a somewhat disorganized band of followers a spirit of unity, courage, and discipline. And nor can we doubt the tremendous influence which it has exercised in the moulding of the Sikh character. Khalsa is an order of 'soldier saints' dedicated to both piety and justice, and pursuing both with a determination, which when necessity compels, may involve the use of the sword. This is the Khalsa ideal and much that we find in subsequent Sikh history is an obvious response to this ideal.

In retrospect it can be aptly concluded that the Five Ks were a fighting man's (soldier's) need and uniform of those stormy times. They were a necessity for fighting, easy movement, and agility; by becoming an integral part of the body they made a man ever ready for action. Above all, the Five Ks were very much essential for identity of the Khalsa and were a paramount and emergent requirement against the atrocities of a monstrous and savage regime, before the whole of north India was made to forcibly adopt the faith of the Arabian prophet. The Khalsa and the Five Ks were an imperative and indispensable requirement to preserve Hinduism and stem the tide of the onslaught of Islam. It was in fact a sine qua non (Latin) – a thing that is absolutely necessary.

By creating the Khalsa, Guru Gobind Singh defied the might of the Mughal Empire. And, in trying to espouse his cause and achieve his goal, he had to fight against heavy odds and make numerous sacrifices. *The only change Guru Gobind Singh brought in religion was to expose the other side of the medal. Whereas Nanak had propagated goodness, Guru Gobind condemned evil. One preached the love of one's neighbour, the other the punishment of transgressors. Nanak's God loved His saints; Gobind's God destroyed His enemies.* (A History of the Sikhs Vol.1 Page 88 by Khushwant Singh).

True, Guru Gobind Singh did not succeed in routing the tyrants who held sway over Hindustan or in liberating Punjab, but he laid the foundation of the Sikh military might by setting up a tradition of reckless valour which became a distinguishing feature of Sikh soldiery. They came to believe in the triumph of their cause as an article of faith, and like their guru asked for no nobler end than death on the battlefield.

With clasped hands this boon I crave
When time comes to end my life
Let me fall in mighty strife.

A hundred years after Guru Gobind Singh founded the Khalsa in 1699, the Sikh Kingdom was established by Maharaja Ranjit Singh in 1799.

**References:**


1. The Encyclopedia of Sikhism – Harbans Singh (Editor-in Chief)
2. Sikhism: Glimpses and Glances (Volume 1) – Bhupender Singh
3. History of the Sikhs and their Religion (Volume 1) – Edited by Kirpal Singh and Kharak Singh (published by SGPC)
4. A History of the Sikhs (Volume 1) – Khushwant Singh
5. A Short History of The Sikhs (Volume 1) – Teja Singh and Ganda Singh
6. The Sikhs and their Scriptures – C H Loehlin

# 5

## HOW THE SIKHS BECAME MILITANT

The first two hundred years of Sikh history from the time Guru Nanak received the divine vision in 1499, to the time Guru Gobind founded the Khalsa in 1699 (Period of the Gurus), can be neatly divided into two equal parts. During the first hundred years (1499-1606) approximately i.e., from the time Guru Nanak was ordained in 1499 till the murder of the fifth Guru Arjun Dev by the Mughals in 1606, the first five Gurus preached an egalitarian, monotheistic, non-idolatrous order, free of meaningless form and ritual. The social order was free of caste distinction and the doors of Sikh temples were thrown open to everyone. The Brahmin and the *Shudra* (untouchable) were to break bread together. It was an eclectic, simple and peaceful reformist movement. No wonder it appealed to one and all (the Hindu and Muslim alike) and moreover it was preached by modest men who laid no claim to kinship with God or garb their utterances as prophecies. They were all holy, humble, peace-loving, and humanitarian men.

In the next hundred years from 1606 (the murder of the fifth Guru Arjan Dev) to 1699 (till the formation of the Khalsa), the Sikhs were forced to become militant in order to fight Mughal tyranny. During this period the masses joined the Sikh ranks to protect themselves and their families and to evade forcible conversions to Islam. This period marked the persecution of the Sikhs. This persecution increased in intensity with the formation of the Khalsa in 1699 and lasted till 1765 (crumbling of the Mughal Empire and ascendancy of the Sikh *misls*). This duration (1699-1765) is referred to as 'The Period of Repression/Persecution'. Thus, the total period of persecution lasted for well over a century and a half.

In 1606 Guru Arjan the fifth Guru was tortured to death. This action of Jahangir was prompted both by religious feelings and political considerations. Guru Arjan was the first Sikh Guru to fall afoul of the Mughal authorities, thus setting the tone for the remaining history of the Mughal Empire. The martyrdom of Guru Arjan Dev was a turning point in the history of the Sikhs and had far reaching consequences. It altered the course of history. After the martyrdom of Guru Arjan the pacific character of Sikhs changed drastically. This event, more than any other, converted the Sikh community into a warrior commonwealth. The supreme sacrifice of the Guru severed the cordial relations between the Sikhs and Mughals, the Sikh religion became more popular, and the Sikhs slowly started following the path of militancy. **Thus, were sown the first seeds of that bitter and implacable enmity** that afterwards came to exist between Muslim and Sikh. As Dr Gokul Chand Narang puts it, "His execution was universally regarded by the Hindus as a sacrifice for their faith. The whole of Punjab began to burn with indignation and revenge."

Guru Arjan stood up against tyranny, terror, and torture unflinchingly. His sacrifice indoctrinated in the Sikhs, the teaching that one must not bow before injustice. By his example, the Sikhs were inspired to follow the path of sacrifice for a just cause with dedication and it also impressed upon them the need for self-defence against tyranny. The first five Gurus were peaceful religious and social reformers; the last five had to take steps to carry on this work against increasingly hostile military forces.

At this point in history, it dawned on the Sikhs that the powerful have no pity and if they wanted peace they had to be prepared for war. They realized that being truthful, good, right, just, peace loving, humane and principled had no value unless it was backed with power. History had proved this, time and time again. The verdict of history has always gone in favour of the powerful. The famous quote of Mao Tse Tung "Power grows out of the barrel of a gun," amply justifies this.

Seeing the war clouds gathering, during his imprisonment the fifth Guru, Arjan asked his son Guru Hargobind to sit fully armed on his throne and to maintain an army of saint-soldiers to face the approaching storm. The Sikhs started taking steps towards becoming belligerent after the execution of their Guru, Arjan Dev and began to change from a pacifist to a militant people. Guru Hargobind built the Sikh community into a military power. He elevated martyrdom to an ideal of the religion; this was not merely dying for the faith but being killed while fighting for the Sikh community. This concept was institutionalized by Guru Hargobind and thereafter Sikhism became a force to be reckoned with. Thus, the second phase of development of Sikh dynamic mysticism started a transition from saint to saint-soldier.

As instructed by his father, the young Guru Hargobind sat on the *Gurugaddi* fully armed with two swords girded around his waist, on his turban he wore the emblem of royalty and was addressed as *Sacha Badshah* (the true king). One sword symbolized spiritual power and the other temporal (***Miri*** – temporal or political and ***Piri*** - spiritual). Henceforth it was a **call to arms**. The Sikhs were asked to bring offerings of arms and horses instead of money and the Sikh community began to actively resist the Mughal Empire and several battles were fought between the two sides. Guru Hargobind had to fight four small battles (skirmishes) that were thrust upon him. The remarkable thing about these battles is that the Guru won all of them and all the four enemy commanders were slain by the Guru in duels. The concept of *Miri* and *Piri* by the sixth Guru changed the Sikh psyche from purely religious to include the military component.

Guru Hargobind had a standing army of eight hundred horses, three hundred horsemen, and sixty foot with firearms and seven guns. He built a small fortress, Lohgarh (castle of steel) at Amritsar. Across the Harmandir, he built the **Akal Takht** (the throne of the Timeless God), where ballads extolling feats of heroism were heard instead of chants of hymns of peace, and military plans discussed instead of religious discourses. The next guru, Har Rai inherited the martial tradition and kept an army of 2,200 horsemen, as advised by his grandfather, but he was essentially a man of peace, and no battle was ever forced on him.

The next major incident that antagonized the Sikhs and made their hackles rise was the most gruesome, cold-blooded murder of their ninth Guru and his three companions. They died to protect the Hindu faith and their refusal to convert to Islam. To curb the increasing power of the Sikhs the Mughal administration ordered the execution of the ninth Guru.

Guru Tegh Bhadur was beheaded on 11 November 1675. This was sheer high handedness on the part of Aurangzeb, the Mughal emperor. The times were such; might was right; Islam was considered the only true religion; the Mughal reigned supreme and did what they liked. Aurangzeb had embarked on a most dastardly path of converting the whole of India into Islam. Human rights and dignity did not exist. The Hindu lived in a miserable condition with untold brutalities and many fold atrocities were committed on him.

Martyrdom of the two Sikh Gurus along with their countless devout Sikhs and the general tyranny of the age brought forth a new determination and vigour to the young nation under the tenth Guru. Guru Gobind was a powerful military general with a profound vision of transforming the suppressed and downtrodden people into an aggressive, warlike society – an absolute necessity for a community surrounded by a hostile and powerful empire. It was now left to Guru Gobind Singh to awaken and unite the people divided among themselves based on caste and creed. Since ages foreign invaders had taken advantage of this division amongst the people of Hindustan. One of the biggest lessons that the British learnt after the Mutiny was to keep the caste divisions intact so that they could divide and rule.

Guru Gobind Singh was a far-sighted man and was looking into the future. It was now for him to arouse and raise the spirits of the meek and timid Hindus and forge a casteless militant fraternity that could fight for its rights. On being confronted by the enemy or when in dire straits, these cowardly and frightened folks, refused to fight back, foregoing their identity and begged their oppressors for mercy. This timidity had to be shed and hence forth the tide reversed. "When all other means have failed, it is righteous to draw the sword," Guru Gobind Singh said, "Light your understanding as a lamp and sweep away the filth of timidity." With this mission in mind, he earnestly set about to "teach the sparrow how to hunt the hawk and one man to have courage to fight a legion."

The Sixth Guru, Hargobind was the first to appeal to arms; the Tenth put the army on a regular footing. It was only after duly considering the given times and conditions, earnestly debating the prevailing situation, profound rumination, and serious deliberation that Guru Gobind decided to form the Khalsa (a brotherhood of saint-soldiers) on *Baisakhi* day, the **29th of March 1699** and bless them with the Five Ks. He roused the dormant warlike instincts of his followers. By making his followers easily recognizable, by virtue of their beards and turbans, the Guru raised a body of fearless warriors who would not be able to deny their faith when in danger. Their external appearance would invite persecution and in turn make them dauntless and thus breed courage to resist it. It was a movement, a revolution, a storm, a blitzkrieg that swept people off their feet.

The Khalsa was in fact a need of the times – a historical necessity. There is no doubt that the creation of the Khalsa is the single most important event in Sikh history. It was an occurrence of great significance and a major turning point in Sikh affairs. It fully unified the community and made it a force to reckon with, militarily. After the formation of the Khalsa, the political and military power of the Sikhs grew tremendously. It heralded the rising of a great people and created lions out of jackals. It gave birth to saint-soldiers; there was many fold increase in the number of Sikhs as the downtrodden and oppressed sections of society were raised to a high status and given a distinct identity. So, there was successful opposition to Mughal rule which finally crumbled and fell. "*The object that the Guru (Gobind Singh) set before himself was to infuse a new life in the dead bones of Hindus to make them forget their differences and present a united front against the tyranny and persecution to which they were exported.*" – G C Narang

As the wave of fanaticism accompanied by oppression was on the rise, the forces of the good and the evil began to array for a showdown. The creation of the Khalsa was not an idle dream. The Khalsa proved its mettle by passing through the ordeal of fire. It is unnecessary to go into details of the struggle, because these are writ large on the pages of Sikh history.

The history of Sikhs after creation of the Khalsa is the saga of an unending series of martyrs and saint-soldiers, who staked their lives for the cause of justice and resistance to oppression and exploitation. The significance of the Khalsa, and the role it played in the revolutionary struggle, are of the utmost importance, because the Khalsa was the climax of the Sikh movement. Suffice it to say that it was this organization of saint-soldiers, which stemmed the spate of invasions from the North-West that had plagued India for nearly a thousand years, and introduced an era of peace, stability, freedom, and human dignity after centuries of tyranny, destruction, slavery, humiliation, and indignity.

Guru Gobind Singh did not succeed in routing the tyrants who held sway over Hindustan, or in liberating the Punjab, but he accomplished much more than that – he liberated the spirit of his people from centuries of apathy and acquiescence. His courage and faith filled the Punjabis with hope and confidence which sustained them during the years of persecution after his death. Shortly before his death (07 October 1708), Guru Gobind Singh selected and entrusted Banda Singh Bahadur with the military command of the Sikhs. He left the task to Banda, of accomplishing by force what appeal to justice had failed to achieve. For seven years (1709 – 1715), Banda played merry hell with the decaying Mughal Empire. He met his Waterloo at Gurdas Nangal in a small fortress called Duni Chand ki Haveli. After Banda Singh Bahadur the persecution of Sikhs started on a large scale and for the first five years after Banda's execution very little was heard of them. The Sikhs again came under sword and fire for another half a century, first by Mughal kings and later by the Afghan King, Ahmad Shah Abdali.

The Khalsa were hunted out of their homes and a price lay on their heads. They scattered in small *jathas* or groups to find refuge in distant hills, forests, and deserts, but they were far from vanquished. Armed with whatever weapons they could lay their hands upon and living off the land, these highly mobile guerilla bands or *jathas* remained active during the worst of times. The Mughals kept hunting them and the Sikhs kept challenging and defying them with determined perseverance. It was at times when the Mughals thought that they had finished the Sikhs, that they rose like the phoenix.

It was during this period that the two *Ghallugharas* (holocausts) took place on 10 March 1746 and 05 February 1762, wherein 10,000 and 35,000 Sikhs (Khalsa) were massacred respectively. The suffering of the Sikhs was tremendous and the mental agony devastating. To live the life of the Khalsa was to be hunted like an animal and was not every one's cup of tea. A vast population of the Hindu faith, during that period, adopted the religion of the Arabian prophet (converted to Islam) as a result of force or with a view to worldly advantage. The majority of Hindus (Sehajdhari Sikhs), who had not joined the Khalsa ranks kept away. This was also the period of the Sikh *misls* (small principalities under feudal war lords) and the *Dal Khalsa*. The Arabic word *misl* means "like" or "equal." The Sikh *misls* were "alike" in the sense that they were considered equals. Their fighting strength was, however, far from equal. Some had only a few hundred men; others, like the Bhangis, could put more than ten thousand soldiers in the field. The *misls* were collectively known as *Dal Khalsa* (Sikh/Khalsa army).

Sikhs from necessity had confederated together and finding that their peaceful deportment did not secure them from oppression, they took up arms to defend themselves against a tyrannical government **as will always happen where the common rights of humanity are violated**. Heroes arose from time to time, whose courage and ability directed the efforts of their injured followers to just though severe revenge. As the progress of these events is related in history, the Sikhs continued to acquire strength. It was this persecution that made the Sikh militants stronger and more resilient; a military power and ultimately enabled them to establish their domination, supremacy, and sovereignty, and finally consummated in their establishing a kingdom and a ruler.

By the turn of the sixteenth century more than half of the population of Punjab had already been converted to Islam and there was no check in sight. The march of Islam from Mecca to convert the whole world was stalled in India by the Sikhs and later Ranjit Singh, the Maharaja of the

Sikhs, not only stemmed the tide of Islam, but also reversed it. It may not be wrong to say that had the Sikhs not taken up the sword, the whole of north India would be reading the Quran today.

Exactly a hundred years after the formation of the Khalsa in 1699, the Sikhs carved out a Kingdom for themselves in 1799, when Ranjit Singh overpowered and united the *misls* (Sikh confederacies or soverign principalities) and was declared the Maharaja of the Punjab and the Khalsa Raj came into existence.

Born therefore, as a peaceful and tolerant religion, Sikhism was gradually transformed from a purely religious movement into a military and political crusade/campaign directed against the weakness and inhumanity of the later Mughal rulers, by the persecutions of fanatical bigots like Aurangzeb and the inhuman brutalities of his weak and debauched successors. **The pursuit of arms and devotion to steel was rendered the religious duty of the Sikhs**. **The Sikhs took to arms in real earnest and thus became militant in the true sense.** There was no looking back now. The Sikhs fought many a battle after this and their fighting qualities and courage and bravery became legendary.

All that the Sikhs are famous for – their valour in battle, their spirit of enterprise, their spirit of camaraderie and their lust for life they owe to this one man – Gobind Singh. If the traditions that the Guru initiated are allowed to die, there is little doubt that the Sikh community will die with them.

**Indeed, the challenge of the Mughal Empire was the turning point in the history of the Sikhs. If the mighty Mughal government had left the Sikhs in peace, free to sing their hymns and to develop their langars, it is quite probable that Sikhism would have remained a comparatively obscure provincial cult. Persecution brought it to the stage of Indian history. Through blood, sweat and tears it walked to political power; the peaceful sect established by Guru Nanak developed into the invincible Khalsa.**

– Dr A C Bannerji

**As a matter of fact, Sikhism grew out of the necessity of suppressing the oppressors. Thousands of simple peasants flocked to the banner of the Khalsa in order to present a united front to the Moslems and wreak vengeance on them for their barbaric, inhuman and intolerant behavior towards a peace-loving people who were quietly and meekly following their faith. It may be said that had the Moslems been tolerant to the Hindus there would have been no Sikhs.**

- Dr A C Banerjee (in his book Anglo-Sikh relations)

**References:**


1. The Encyclopedia of Sikhism – Harbans Singh (Editor-in Chief)
2. Sikhism: Glimpses and Glances (Volume 1) – Bhupender Singh
3. History of the Sikhs and their Religion (Volume 1) – Edited by Kirpal Singh and Kharak Singh (published by SGPC)
4. A History of the Sikhs (Volume 1) – Khushwant Singh
5. A Short History of The Sikhs (Volume 1) – Teja Singh and Ganda Singh
6. Sikhism (Its Philosophy and History) - Edited by Daljeet Singh and Kharak Singh (published by Institute of Sikh Studies)
7. The Sikhs and their Scriptures – C H Loehlin
8. Internet (Wikipedia, the free encyclopedia)

# 6

# A BRIEF ACCOUNT OF THE BATTLES OF GURU GOBIND SINGH

Guru Gobind fought fourteen; some historians say sixteen and still others twenty battles (big and small). They are all right in their own way. If we consider all the battles (big and small), skirmishes, scuffles and squabbles, the sum comes to twenty. The Guru fought six battles during the pre-Khalsa period (1675 - 1699) and fourteen battles in the post Khalsa period (1699 - 1708). Out of these twenty battles, the Guru lost only two of them (these two military reverses suffered by the Guru were terrible and cost him heavily).

The hill chiefs considered the emergence of Khalsa as a potent threat to their authority and established values and a direct challenge to their feudal order and style of living. The main reasons for the opposition of the hill rajas to the Guru were that they considered Guru Gobind a threat because of his growing power in their region, they had ideological differences (caste system and social equality, rituals and idol worship), which led to increasing insubordination of the lower castes, who had begun to turn to the casteless Sikh fraternity for leadership, the danger and fear of reprisal of the Mughal power at Delhi, instigation by the Mughals, and lastly their opportunism. Thus, it was a more or less love hate relationship with them.

## Battles during the pre Khalsa period (1675 - 1699)

**1. Battle of Bhangani 1686.** Guru Gobind's first baptism in steel was in the battle of Bhangani (1686) against the combined forces of the hill chiefs and Pathans (mercenaries in the Sikh army who were won over by the hill rajas). Despite the desertions and numerical superiority of the enemy, the Sikhs (most of whom were Hindus of the trading castes) carried the day. It was in this battle that Pir Buddhu Shah lost his brother, two sons and many of his disciples. The victory at Bhangani gave confidence to the young Guru to return to Anandpur.

**2. Battle of Nadaun 1687.** The Guru's second battle was fought at Nadaun (1687). This time it was the hill rajas who had requested the Guru to lead them against the Mughals, led by Alif Khan. The initial round was won by the confederates. Despite the victory the hill chiefs decided to come to terms with the Mughal commander to avoid the likelihood of another force being sent against them. Guru Gobind kept aloof and refused to enter into these discussions.

**3. Khanzada's Expedition 1694.** Dilawar Khan, the faujdar (in Mughal times an office that combined the functions of a military commander along with judicial and land revenue functions) of Kangra was instructed to curb the growing power of Guru Gobind Singh. The faujdar sent an army against the Guru under the command of his son Khanzada Rustam Khan. Khanzada planned to make a sudden, surprise attack on the Sikhs under cover of darkness. The Guru's *deorhidar* (Chamberlain), Alam Khan detected the movement of the enemy and alerted the Guru. Immediately, *Ranjit Nagara* (literally, 'Battle winning Drum') was sounded. The quick formations of the Sikhs bewildered the foe, and the guns of the Khalsa which began to discharge volleys of murderous shot, completely terrified the enemy. They were forced to retire with their weapons unused and return to Dilawar Khan crestfallen. Thus, the Guru was victorious without much fight. Many of Khanzada's soldiers lost their lives while crossing the flooded ravine. The Sikhs, up to this day call the ravine by the name of Himayati Nala – 'the helpful brook.'

**4. Hussain Khan's Expedition 1695.** The failure of Khanzada piqued Dilawar Khan and he sent another expedition under Hussain Khan. Bhim Chand, the ruler of Kahlur (Bilaspur) and Kirpal Chand, the ruler of Katoch joined hands with Hussain Khan. The combined force made plans to march to Anandpur. But en route Hussain Khan got embroiled with Gopal the raja of Guler. Thus, the force which was sent against the Guru got caught in another dispute. Gopal was attacked and, in his helplessness he approached Guru Gobind, who sent 300 Sikhs for his help. A bloody battle was fought in which the enemy was trounced and Hussain Khan and Kirpal Chand with many of their soldiers were killed. In this way, Gopal won the battle and the Guru remarked that the rain of bullets that was originally intended for him was showered by the almighty elsewhere. Guru Gobind calls this battle '*The Hussaini War*'.

**5. Expedition of Jujhar Singh and Chandan Rai 1695.** Dilawar Khan sent yet another expedition under Jujhar Singh and Chandan Rai. They were sent to Jaswan, but they could not achieve the purpose. They recovered Bhalan, fourteen kilometers from Anandpur, a strategic place in the state, which had previously been captured by the hill chiefs and was now in the charge of a Jaswan contingent. But before they could proceed further, they were attacked by Gaj Singh of Jaswan. Jujhar Singh and Chandan Rai put up a brave and determined fight but were soon overpowered. Jujhar Singh was killed in action and Chandan Rai fled. The enemy failed to reach Anandpur.

**6. Prince Muazzam's (Bahadur Shah's) Expedition 1696**. Aurangzeb, who was in southern India to extend his sovereignty over the Shia states and the Marathas realized the gravity of the situation and the loss to the government exchequer. The Mughal administration in the hill states fell in disarray, the hill rajas withheld payment of their annual tributes in defiance of their agreements; the Sikhs were emboldened and their attitude towards the imperial authorities hardened. In this grave and disturbing situation, Aurangzeb realized that drastic action had to be taken. He ordered his son prince Muazzam later **Emperor Bahadur Shah** (1643 – 1712) to take out a punitive expedition for the restoration of law and order and recovery of unpaid tribute.

Muazzam took position in Lahore and from there directed operations against the hill rajas. He deputed Mirza Beg to teach a lesson to the hill chiefs. The general inflicted defeat after defeat, plundered their country, set fire to villages, took hundreds of prisoners, and made examples of the rajas by shaving them clean, blackening their faces, seating them on donkeys and marching them throughout the disturbed area.

Amidst all this the Guru was not touched though he had prepared himself to meet any contingency. Mirza Beg had secret instructions not to bother the Guru (as per Sikh chronicles this was brought about by the good offices of one Nand Lal "Goya," a Sahajdhari Sikh poet of Persian, who had influence over the prince). The prince was looking into the future and Realpolitik dictated to him, what he should do under the circumstances. The prince saw that the Guru had a totally dedicated following that would come in handy during the war for succession which was imminent (the Guru came to his support in the battle of succession). As a result, Guru Gobind was left unmolested for about twelve years after the battle of Nadaun.

## Battles of Post Khalsa Period (1699-1708)

**1. Attack while hunting**. Two chieftains of the hill states, Alim Chand and Balia Chand attacked Guru Gobind Singh when he was out hunting with a few Sikhs. The Sikhs gave a determined fight, but because of their numerical inferiority, they soon started losing ground. However, reinforcement under Bhai Udai Singh arrived and turned the tables. Alim Chand lost his right arm and fled the field. Balia Chand was seriously wounded and all the enemy soldiers took to their heels. The Guru and his men returned victorious.

**2. Prelude to First Battle of Anandpur**. The aforementioned defeat unnerved the hill rajas and they sought the help of the Mughal government. According to MA Macauliffe, on the instructions of Aurangzeb, the *subedar* of Delhi dispatched a force of ten thousand soldiers under two able generals, Painda Khan (not to be mistaken with Painda Khan of Guru Hargobind's time) and Din Beg. The hill chiefs joined them at Ropar and the combined force marched towards Anandpur. In the clash of arms near Anandpur, Painda Khan died and the remaining army fled. They were pursued for some distance by the Khalsa soldiers and a large booty comprising horses, arms and baggage fell into the hands of the Sikhs.

**3. First Battle of Anandpur 1700**. The crestfallen hill chiefs now decided to take on the Guru minus the Mughals. They came together and gave command to Ajmer Chand, son of Bhim Chand of Bilaspur because of the location of Guru Gobind's headquarters in his state. Ajmer Chand sent a message to the Guru that he should vacate Anandpur or pay taxes thereof, failing which he would have to face the raja's wrath. The threat/demand was rejected forthwith, and the Guru sent fiats to his followers to come to Anandpur at the earliest to face the war that was in the offing. The Sikhs took positions in their forts, predominantly Anandgarh, Fatehgarh and Kesgarh.

On 28 July 1700, Ajmer Chand made a forceful attack on Taragarh, near Anandgarh, but was repulsed by Sahibzada Ajit Singh. Next day, Ajmer Chand again mounted a fierce assault on Fatehgarh fort. He and his allies met with stout resistance, and in the dogged sallies organized by veteran Bhagwan Singh and the Sikhs under his command, they suffered heavy casualties in a five-hour battle. At sunset, fighting stopped; along with other Sikhs, Bhagwan Singh and Jawhar Singh fell on this day. On the following day with the advent of dawn, fighting resumed. Ajmer Chand launched a vigorous attack, this time on Agamgarh, but failed miserably. Two prominent Sikh leaders, Bhag Singh and Gharbar Singh lost their lives.

At an enemy council meeting to take stock of the situation, it was decided that to begin with, the fort of Lohgarh should be stormed to be followed by simultaneous attacks on other sides of Anandpur. The leadership of the forces meant to storm Lohgarh was given to a very brave and daring chieftain, Kesri Chand Jaswaria. One of the meticulously planned manoeuvres was to set a highly intoxicated elephant against the door of Lohgarh to break into the fort. The plan though made in camera, leaked out. The Guru appointed Dhuni Chand (considered to be a bold and mentally robust man) to confront the animal, but when he chickened out Bachittar Singh, son of Mani Singh, lost no time in offering his services to the Guru. Guru Gobind gave him a *nagni* (spear) with which to face the inebriated pachyderm.

As the day of the attack dawned, the hill forces under the overall command of Ajmer Chand positioned themselves near the fort of Lohgarh, while the troops of Kesri Chand drove the sozzled and infuriated elephant towards the main gate of the fort. When the furious animal advanced to strike the door, Bachittar Singh struck it with such force that his spear pierced through the plates covering its forehead, to the brain that it turned around and ran helter-skelter trampling all that came in its way including the enemy soldiers. In the disorder that ensued, Udai Singh, already astride his swift horse, sprang forward and challenged Kesri Chand. Kesri Chand seated on his horse attacked with his sword, Udai Singh swung aside and then with a sudden, forceful blow with his sword cut Kesri Chand into two pieces. Kesri Chand having met his nemesis, Ajmer Chand thought it prudent to seek safety in retreat.

Fighting continued for four consecutive days but did not yield any fruitful results for the hill rulers and they looked for a truce. The shrewd and cunning, Pandit Parmanand, the family priest of the raja of Kahlur came to the rescue of the hill chiefs. In a very stealthy and subtle way, he placed a letter tied to the idol of a cow with a *janeu* (a sacred thread or cord) at the gate of Anandpur. The contents of the letter said that the *rajas* sincerely regretted the loss of life on both sides and desired an immediate settlement, so that the purposeless hostilities came to an end. The letter also stated that a unilateral retreat on their part would be too humiliating and mortifying, and that if the Guru vacated Anandpur, the siege would be raised and then he could come back after some time, if he desired. They appealed to the Gurus sense of chivalry by requesting him to leave Anandpur to them as the *gau-bhet*, i.e. "the gift of the holy mother cow." The Guru agreed expecting that the hill chiefs had realized the futility of waging war.

**4. Battle of Nirmohgarh 1700**. Leaving Anandpur in the hands of some brave and trusted men, the Guru came out in the open ground and established himself at Nirmohgarh, four kilometers from Anandpur. The hill chiefs throwing their promises to the winds again attacked the Sikhs. The Sikhs resisted and after a vigorous assault, the hill chiefs had to lift the siege. Ajmer Chand, now decided to end the matter once and for all and he sought assistance from the Mughal government. The Mughal contingents and the hill army arrived at Sirhind. From there the combined army of the Mughal, Sirhind and hill rajas moved for the operation.

Guru Gobind was well aware of the situation and was abreast of circumstances, and he had made thorough preparation for the eventualities of the future. The allied forces attacked from one side and Ajmer Chand from the other. The contest lasted for about a day before the Khalsa could get some respite from the enemy's vigorous attack. Ultimately, Guru Gobind Singh was constrained to evacuate Nirmohgarh, probably because of the use of cannons by the Mughal *faujdar*. But before they could cross the Sutlej River they were overtaken by the enemy and the Khalsa fought desperately for four hours and eventually succeeded in crossing the river and entering the territory of Raja Dharampal, the chief of Jaswan, who was a friend, admirer and well-wisher of the Guru. Guru Gobind Singh along with his Khalsa marched towards the town of Basohli.

**5. Battle of Basohli 1700**. The Sikhs had hardly left the place when another engagement took place on the further banks of River Sutlej. The Khalsa fought gallantly and repelled this attack. In the mean while the fighting elements of the enemy army crossed the river and assaulted the Guru's army at Basohli. The Sikhs put up a formidable defence and once again the enemy was unable to subdue them.

The loss of life and property on both sides was heavy and the hill rajas and Mughal troops went back to their respective territories with the satisfaction of having achieved, although at a very high cost a limited objective of expelling the Khalsa from the territory of Kahlur on the eastern side of the Sutlej.

The Guru stayed at Basohli for some days, and then took the initiative against Ajmer Chand, leading incursions on the north of River Sutlej and gradually moving towards Anandpur. Finally, he entered Anandpur and lost no time in repairing the forts and other buildings badly damaged by the hill soldiery.

**6. Second Battle of Anandpur 1701.** Soon Anandpur was functioning in full glory as the headquarters of the Khalsa. Towards the end of 1700, the peace at Anandpur was again disturbed with a surprise attack by Wazir Khan, the *subedar* of Sirhind. The Sikhs had to evacuate the city and move to Bhadsali, 45 km from Anandpur beyond Una, across River Swan. The Mughal army went in pursuit and engaged the Khalsa. In the hard-fought battle, the Sikhs emerged victorious. Soon after, when everything was quiet, the Guru returned to Anandpur to resume activities and increase his area of influence.

**7. Third Battle of Anandpur 1702**. In 1702, Sayyed Beg and Alif Khan, two eminent commanders of the Mughals on their way to Delhi from Lahore were tempted by Ajmer Chand to attack Anandpur by offering a huge sum of money. Both the commanders marched towards Anandpur, but after a few skirmishes, **Sayyed Beg** was so impressed by the Guru's charismatic personality that he thought it appropriate to join the Guru. Alif Khan had to retire in spite of his long-cherished desire to avenge his failure which he had met earlier in the Battle of Naudhan, in the Kangra hills.

**8 and 9. Fourth and Fifth Battles of Anandpur 1703 - 04**. In 1703, there were two campaigns against the Guru, both plotted by Ajmer Chand. During the first operation his allies were Bhup Chand, Wazir Singh and Dev Saran and on the second occasion, he sought support from the *subedar* of Delhi. On both occasions he suffered defeat. In the second battle, during an attack a remarkable thing happened, **Maimun Khan**, a Mughal commander deserted his side and joined the Guru in response to the call of his conscience. In this action one hill chief and **Sayyed Beg** (fighting for the Guru) were killed. The enemy forces fought with utmost gallantry that they drove the Sikhs out of Anandpur and plundered the town. Soon after, the Khalsa returned, fell upon the heavily laden enemy troops, retrieved their possessions, and recovered Anandpur.

**10. Sixth Battle of Anandpur May 1705.** After some time, hostilities resumed and led to the Sixth Battle of Anandpur. This time, the hill chiefs made a formidable combination against the Guru and proceeded to attack Anandpur, they encountered heavy artillery fire. In order to avert heavy casualties, the enemy decided to lay siege to the town instead of suffering great losses and the other consequences of attacking. But the sorties and raids of the Khalsa cavalry ruined this plan too, so they had no alternative, except immediate withdrawal.

Despite this the hill men never relented in their determined resolve to oust the Guru from their territory. They prepared on a grand scale; the Gujjars and Ranghars were incited to join hands with them; they harnessed their resources with meticulous care and got assistance of troops from Lahore and Sirhind. The allied forces attacked Anandpur, but the Khalsa soldiers got the better of them and they were driven out of Anandpur. Then the allies encircled the Sikhs on all sides and the great siege of Anandpur began.

Guru Gobind also made counter plans to this move of the enemy. He issued several letters to various Sikh *sangats* (a fellowship or assembly, especially a local Sikh community or congregation), asking them for reinforcements and divided his army into six contingents with one each in the five forts and a detachment of 500 men kept in reserve. Sahibzada Ajit Singh, who headed the troops at Keshgarh Fort, won a great victory on the very first day by knocking off Jagatullah, leader of the Gujjars and Ranghars. Two heavy guns named *Baghan* (Tigress) and *Vijay Gosh* (Victory Warrant) were nominated for Anandgarh. They wrought havoc in the enemy ranks. In the first day's fight, Wazir Khan lost nine hundred men.

The siege was strengthened and conducted with great intensity. It was planned in such a manner that all ingress and egress for goods and personnel were blocked. The situation for the Khalsa became very precarious and they were driven to undertake very dangerous missions to raid provision stores. They only encountered partial success and that too on some occasions. After this the allies collected their stores at one place and guarded them day and night. The Sikhs resorted to direct assaults on the enemy, but they mostly failed. A small hill channel from Charan Ganga, supplying water to Anandpur was diverted by the Kallur raja from its course, thus adding more misery to the Khalsa.

The Sikhs started breaking down from hunger and thirst and under extreme hardship requested the Guru to vacate the fort. Guru Gobind advised patience for some more time and told them that anyone who wanted to leave was free to do so. From previous knowledge and incidents, the Guru did not trust the enemy and knew that the enemy promises of safe passage, even on the Quran would never be fulfilled and he proved it to the Sikhs. The Khalsa was under dire straits; forty Sikhs (later known as the *Chali muktas or* the emancipated ones) from Moga deserted the Guru. The adversary knew that the Guru would never surrender, and the Guru's decision was prompted more by his determination to die fighting than by the promises held out to him by the hill chiefs and Mughals.

Ultimately, against his wish and better judgment, Guru Gobind decided to vacate Anandpur on night 5/6 December 1705.

**11. Battle of Shahi Tibbi.** On the night of **5/6 December** 1705, Guru Gobind Singh left Anandpur. The moment the enemy got an inkling of the departure of the Sikhs, they forgot their vows and set out in hot pursuit. Skirmishes commenced from Kiratpur onwards. Realising the impending danger, Guru Gobind Singh gave a band of 50 Sikhs to Bhai Udai Singh with the responsibility of checking the enemy's advance. At Shahi Tibbi, the small band of fifty Sikhs under **Udai Singh** fell back and fought a bloody battle with the enemy. They held the enemy until they were killed to a man. This was a delaying or rearguard action and the battle lasted for two and a half hours.

**12. Battle of Sarsa bank**. When the battle of Shahi Tibbi was in progress, the rest of the caravan including the Guru had reached the bank of Sarsa River. It was almost first light now, on **06 December**. About this time news arrived that a contingent of enemy troops was fast approaching. Bhai Jiwan Singh, a prominent Sikh, who had brought the severed head of Guru Tegh Bahadur to Guru Gobind in Anandpur, along with 100 Sikhs was asked to encounter the enemy. When the enemy caught up with the Guru's caravan, close to the banks of River Sarsa, Bhai Jiwan Singh Rangreta (1649-1705) with his hundred men fought another rearguard action to harass and delay the pursuers. While crossing River Sarsa, which was in spate many Sikh soldiers were swept away and many drowned in the river. There was great loss to valuable literature and property.

**13. Battle of Chamkaur (07 December 1705)**

The two rearguard actions gave the Guru time to reach Chamkaur, where he and forty men who were left with him built a stockade and decided to fight to a finish. The local *zamindar* (landlord) of the place invited the Guru to come to the village and put his mud *haveli* (mansion), also called *garhi* (mud fortess) by locals, at the disposal of the Guru.

The Guru's force comprised forty men besides him and his two elder sons (forty-three in all). Heavily outnumbered, the gallant little band kept the enemy at bay. Every few hours some of them would rush out and fight to the end. Ultimately only five of the forty remained. The Guru too would have lost his life in this battle had these five Singhs not ordered him to flee the battleground. Out of these five, two remained behind to continue the struggle. When all seemed lost, a Sikh (Sangat Singh) who resembled the Guru put on his dress and went out to fight. While the enemy was celebrating their kill, the Guru and the three Sikhs made good their escape.

The Battle of Chamkaur (07 December 1705) was literally and metaphorically a great 'last stand'. A great saga of bravery had been enacted. However, since it was a literal fight to the finish there is no doubt that all that can be imagined in terms of individual and collective bravery and human emotions would have been enacted.

It was the most crucial battle and the biggest debacle/reverse that Guru Gobind Singh faced in his whole military career. He was besieged by an overwhelming enemy and the odds, in terms of strength (forty-three men versus a legion), resources, weapons and ground were heavily poised against him. The Guru lost two of his elder sons (Ajit Singh and Jujhar Singh), three of the *Panj Piare* – Five Beloved Ones (Himmat Singh, Mohkam Singh and Sahib Singh), Pandit Kirpa Ram (Singh) and thirty-three of his beloveds, stalwart Sikhs (the names of many famous Sikh warriors are included amongst these), besides the ones mentioned earlier. Ultimately, only the Guru and three Singhs survived. The three Sikhs included Maan Singh and two of the Five Beloved Ones (Daya Singh and Dharam Singh). A greater study on the battle by military experts is required.

**14. Battle of Khidrana or Muktsar (29 December 1705).** In the winter of 1705, Guru Gobind Sigh was in Dhilwan (Ferozpur District) when he received intelligence of Wazir Khan marching against him. The men under the Guru were not strong enough to face Wazir Khan. They were few and lacked sufficient arms and munitions. The Guru thought of seeking safety in the forests of Khidrana in the interior of the Malwa desert. Except for one large pool, there was no water for miles around Khidrana. If the Sikhs took possession of the water body before Wazir Khan's men caught up with them, the strain of battle in the sweltering afternoon heat would soon force the 'Turks' to give up the fight and instead go in search of water.

On reaching Khidrana, the Sikhs found the tank dry. The Sirhind army was hot on their heels. Guru Gobind entrenched his men on a sandy hill, miles from the forest. In this desperate situation help was godsend; it came unexpected. A band of horsemen rode up to the entrenchment. They were the forty men who had deserted the Guru during the siege of Anandpur. When they heard of the Guru's predicament, they felt ashamed and left their homes to redeem themselves. They reached Khidrana a little ahead of Wazir Khan's troops and swore to hold the 'Turks' before they got to the Guru.

To deceive the enemy of their strength the Sikhs draped bushes with clothes. The ruse only invited a heavier attack from the 'Turks'. The Sikhs had little gunpowder. They emerged from their hideout and engaged the enemy in hand-to-hand combat. The small band was overpowered; they fell fighting to the last man. They were the saviours.

Wazir Khan was convinced that he had seen the last of the Guru and his Sikhs. He ordered his men to search the battlefield for the Guru's body. But the heat was intense, and the thirsty soldiers soon gave up the quest to return to the village.

After waiting all day on the sandy hill, Guru Gobind rode down towards the forest. He discovered why the enemy had failed to reach him. He recognized the mutilated bodies which littered the battlefield. Only one of the Sikhs, Mahan Singh was alive. He craved forgiveness for himself and his comrades for having deserted the Guru at Anandpur. Guru Gobind Singh tore up the deed of renunciation and as tribute to the martyrs named the tank of Khidrana *Muktsar* – the "Pool of Salvation." Hence the Battle of Khidrana is also known as the Battle of Muktsar.

From the aforementioned account of the battles, it will be seen that it was a 'war of attrition.' The Guru lost his entire army in the twenty battles that he fought. After the Battle of Chamkaur, he was left with only three men. The biggest problem that Guru Gobind faced was to keep his men motivated and inspired at all times.

What was it that made Guru Gobind's men die readily for him, have full confidence in him and give total dedication to him and his cause? The biggest asset that the Guru had was his superb leadership. Guru Gobind Singh had a keen insight into human nature and was an adept and admirable leader. He led by example and despite all odds, gave victories to his soldiers and that is the best way a leader can gain the confidence of his men. A very important quality of the Guru's splendid personality was his equipoise and unity of purpose. Nothing could move him from his chosen path. His sincerity, military competence, hard work and dedication were of a very high order. He led from the front, lived with his troops, shared their difficulties, hopes and sorrows, and considered it his solemn duty to protect and look after his soldiers. He sacrificed all that he had. Above all, in everything he wrote or spoke, or did there was a note of buoyant hope (*chardi kala*) and the conviction that even if he lost his life, his mission was bound to succeed.

Another vital factor was the unity of purpose and the training and fighting skills that Guru Gobind imparted to his men because it is the man behind the weapon that counts. He also imbibed martial qualities (bravery, loyalty, devotion, grit, determination, perseverance, and sincerity) in his fiery troops and used poetry in rousing their drooping spirits. All this added to the achievements of the Guru. Martyrdom was basic to the Sikh faith and the high value placed on martyrdom in the Sikh religion is evident from the fact that all Sikhs remember their innumerable martyrs in daily *ardaas* (a prayer to God). These factors instilled a high quality of discipline, morale, esprit de corps, and efficiency in his men.

References:


1. The Encyclopedia of Sikhism – Harbans Singh (Editor-in Chief)
2. Sikhism: Glimpses and Glances (Volume 1) – Bhupender Singh
3. History of the Sikhs and their Religion (Volume 1) – Edited by Kirpal Singh and Kharak Singh (published by SGPC)
4. A History of the Sikhs (Volume 1) – Khushwant Singh
5. Martyrdom in Sikhism – Edited by Kharak Singh (IOSS Chandigarh)
6. Internet (Wikipedia, the free encyclopedia)

# 7

## SACRIFICES OF GURU GOBIND SINGH

Guru Gobind Singh was an embodiment of courage and sacrifice; his whole life was a unique example of unparalleled sacrifices; in order to fight against injustice and tyranny, he raised his voice and sacrificed all the comforts of life. More than a military or political leader, Guru Gobind was essentially a man of God with character and integrity. His inspiration came from the strong moral values and ethics ingrained in him by his parents and ancestors and the scriptures that had come down to him through the generations from the time of Baba Nanak. All scriptures are profitable for correction and instruction in righteousness, so that God's man may be complete, thoroughly equipped for every good work and sacrifice.

Guru Nanak's teachings became an instrument of social change and gave roots to a socio-religious movement, and it led to political developments that turned the course of history. It created an awakening that had an impact beyond the times of Nanak, into the future. It enabled Guru Gobind Singh nearly a century and a half later in 1699, to transform an oppressed and helpless people to the leonine (resembling lions) men of the Khalsa.

There is no doubt that the creation of the Khalsa is the single most important event in the annals of the Sikh people. It was an occurrence of great significance and a major turning point in Sikh history. It did away with the caste system; fully unified the community and made it a force to reckon with militarily. After the formation of the Khalsa, the political and military power of the Sikhs grew tremendously. It heralded the rising of a great people and created lions out of jackals. It gave birth to saint-soldiers; there was many fold increase in the number of Sikhs as the downtrodden and oppressed sections of society were raised to a high status and given a distinct identity. So, there was successful opposition to Mughal rule which finally crumbled and fell.

The history of Sikhs after creation of the Khalsa is the story of an unending series of saint-soldiers, sacrifices and martyrs, who staked their lives for the cause of justice and resistance to oppression and exploitation, and the remaining life of Guru Gobind Singh was spent in fighting battles. The significance of the Khalsa, and the role it played in the revolutionary struggle, are of the highest importance, because the Khalsa was the climax of the Sikh movement. Suffice it to say that it was this organization of saint-soldiers, which stemmed the spate of invasions from the North-West that had plagued India for nearly a thousand years, and introduced an era of peace, stability, freedom, and human dignity after centuries of tyranny, destruction, slavery, humiliation, and indignity.

How did Guru Gobind Singh create a culture of such integrity? The Sikh scriptures played a sterling role and made the Guru's task easier. Transforming a nation requires cultivating character. They need hearts and minds that are transformed by God's word and spirit. That is why God gave us the religious scriptures. And, there was the Guru's superb leadership, splendid personality, equipoise and unity of purpose. His sincerity, military competence, hard work and dedication were also of a very high order.

On 25 May 1675, a deputation of sixteen Kashmiri Brahmins, headed by **Kirpa Ram** reached Anandpur. They waited on the Guru and apprised him of Aurangzeb's religious apartheid, persecution, and fanaticism and how he was converting the Kashmiris to Islam. After days of cogitation, Guru Tegh Bahadur told the pundit delegation from Kashmir, that if a man of piety was prepared to defy Sher Afghan (the governor of Kashmir) at the risk of his life, the Hindus could be saved. The assembly was silent till Gobind Rai (eight years of age) asked: "Who could be more pious than the Guru?" Guru Tegh Bahadur made up his mind and he told the pundits to inform the governor that if he could convert their Guru, Tegh Bahadur to his creed, the Hindus of Kashmir would offer no further resistance. Sher Afghan consulted the viceroy at Delhi, who summoned the Guru to his presence. Ultimately the Guru made the supreme sacrifice on 11 November 1675.

Guru Gobind Rai was only nine years old on **11 November 1675** when he became the Guru**.** In the sudden storm that followed Guru Tegh Bahadur's beheading, **Bhai Lakhi shah Vanjara** lifted the dead body in one of his bullock carts and brought it to his hut in village Raisina. Here a pyre was prepared, and the hut set on fire. **Gurdwara Rikab Ganj** (near Rashtrapati Bhawan, New Delhi) stands on this site, today. The head was lifted by a devout Sikh, **Bhai Jaita (Jiwan Singh Rangreta)** and carried to Anandpur Sahib. The shock to the child Guru's mind and to other members of the family need not be exaggerated. The place where the head was cremated in Anandpur is also called **Sis Ganj**.

Guru Gobind Singh had to start from scratch, and he had an uphill task all the way. He had to fight against Muslim officers and Hindu rajas who were directed by Aurangzeb to co-operate with imperial troops in putting down the rebellious Sikhs. The Guru defeated them more than once and his following went on increasing. The Guru's home at Anandpur was besieged five times and eventually he had to abandon this place and take refuge in the plains. He was pursued by the Mughals and hunted from place to place and had to escape to the *Daknin* (South) through Bikaner. Two of his sons were slain during the course of fighting and the remaining two were put to death by the *faujdar* of Sirhind (1705).

### **Week of Sacrifices and Martyrdom** (6-13 December 1705)

On the night of **5/6 December** 1705, Guru Gobind Singh vacated Anandpur. The moment the enemy got an inkling of the departure of the Sikhs, they forgot their vows and set out in hot pursuit. Skirmishes commenced from Kiratpur onwards. At Shahi Tibbi a small band of fifty Sikhs under **Udai Singh** fell back and held the enemy until they were killed to a man. It was almost first light, on **06 December**, when the enemy caught up with the Guru's caravan, close to the banks of River Sarsa. Bhai Jiwan Singh Rangreta (1649-1705) with a hundred men fought another action to harass and delay the pursuers.

From the time gained by these two rearguard actions, the Guru was able to descend into the flooded waters of the Sarsa with the rest of his people. While crossing River Sarsa, which was in spate many Sikh soldiers were swept away and many drowned in the river. There was great loss to valuable literature and property. The Guru's mother and two younger sons got separated; they were taken by their cook, Gangu Brahmin to his village Kheri (a village, 2 km west of Morinda in Ropar district of Punjab). His two wives (Mata Sundar Kaur and Mata Sahib Kaur) were hurriedly led by Bhai Mani Singh to the house of Jawhar Singh at Delhi (the place now houses the **Mata Sundri College**). The Guru reached Chamkaur via village Ghanaula and Kotla Nihang Khan, on the night of **06 December** 1705.

At Chamkaur, the local *zamidar* (landlord) put his mud *haveli* called *garhi* (mud fortress) at Guru Gobind Singh's disposal. The Guru, along with his two elder sons and forty Sikhs who were left with him built a stockade (barrier or enclosure) and decided to fight to a finish. On **07 December** 1705 was fought the Battle of Chamkaur. The gallant little band kept the enemy at bay. Every few hours, some of them would rush out and fight to the finish. Ultimately only five of the forty remained. The five Sikhs ordered the Guru to leave. Two Sikhs, Sant Singh and Sangat Singh remained behind and the other three were also asked to escape from Chamkaur. When all seemed lost, a Sikh (Sangat Singh) who resembled the Guru put on his dress and went out to fight. While the enemy was celebrating their kill, the Guru and the three Sikhs made good their escape. This happened on the night of **7/8 December** 1705.

Guru Gobind fought sixteen battles (big and small). The biggest debacle/reverse that he faced in his whole military career was in the Battle of Chamkaur (07 December 1705). He was besieged by an overwhelming enemy and the odds, in terms of strength, resources, weapons and ground were heavily against him. Among those who fell at Chamkaur were the Guru's two elder sons (Ajit Singh and Jujhar Singh), three of the *Panj Piare* – Five Beloved Ones (Himmat Singh, Mokham Singh and Sahib Singh), Pandit Kirpa Ram (Singh), Bhai Jaita (Jiwan Singh Rangreta) and thirty-two of his beloveds, stalwart Sikhs (the names of many famous Sikh warriors are included amongst these), besides the ones mentioned earlier. Only the Guru and three Sikhs survived. The three Sikhs included Maan Singh and two of the Five Beloved Ones (Daya Singh and Dharam Singh).

The Guru's journey towards Malwa Desert is a saga of fortitude and suffering. At Machiwara two Pathans, **Nabi Khan** and **Ghani Khan**, whom the Guru had known earlier, saved his life. They put the Guru in a curtained palanquin and passed the Mughal sentries with the explanation that they were carrying their *pir* (*Uch da Pir*). That was the end of the pursuit as far as the Guru was concerned. He then arrived at the village of Jatpura.

Gangu, for the love of mammon, treacherously betrayed the two small sons and mother (Mata Gujri) of the Guru, to the local Muslim officer. They were arrested on **08 December** and confined to Sirhind Fort in the *Thanda Burj* (Cold Tower). Finally on **12 December**, the two small boys were executed on the orders of Wazir Khan, the governor of Sirhind and Mata Gujri died the same day. Two august gentlemen, Seth Todar Mall and Moti Ram Mehra conducted their funeral on **13 December** 1705. Gangu's village, Kheri, was destroyed by Banda Singh Bahadur in 1710, and the habitation that reappeared on its ruins dropped the old name, Kheri and adopted the new name of Saheri.

**Beyond Chamkaur**

After escaping from the battlefield of Chamkaur, the Guru with three companions went towards Machhiwara, braving indescribable risks and suffering from fatigue, hunger, and exhaustion, he reached Macchiwara, bare-footed. He was dead tired; his feet were swollen and full of blisters; living in disguise, he survived on leaves of trees and forest fruit with the Mughal army in hot pursuit. He then arrived in the village of Jatpura, weary of limb but still full of faith and courage. It is probable that Guru Gobind Singh composed his famous lines *hal muridan da kehna* in a mood of despondency about this time. The poem is one of the very few that he wrote in Punjabi.

> Beloved friend, beloved God, Thou must hear
> Thy servant's plight when Thou art not near.
> The comforts' cloak is a pall of pest,

The home is like a serpent's nest.
The wine chokes like a hangman's noose,
The rim of the goblet is like an assassin's knife,
But with Thee shall I in adversity dwell,
Without Thee life in ease is life in hell.

Sabad Hazare

The history of the world has not known another family where so many of its members sacrificed themselves for the love of their country, where everything was willingly offered for the sake of the poor and downtrodden. Guru Gobind Singh's great grandfather, Guru Arjan, was mercilessly tortured to death on the banks of the River Ravi. His grandfather Guru Hargobind was captured and incarcerated in Gwalior Fort, in MP; his father, Guru Tegh Bahadur, was beheaded in Chandni Chowk, Delhi; his nephew Guru Har Krishan succumbed to smallpox while tending to the sick and dying; Guru Gobind Singh himself was the victim of a hired assassin's dagger at Nanded (Maharashtra); two sons, Ajit and Jhujhar (17 and 15 years old) fought valiantly and died fighting at Chamkaur; the two younger sons Zorawar and Fateh Singh (9 and 7 years old) were bricked alive at Sirhind; and everyone, near and dear including his mother, wife, uncles and adherents, were sacrificed to serve the cause that he had espoused. He left no cash, no property, no heir to succeed him and no claimant to ask for office. He abolished succession by heredity, and restored to the people, for the first time in man's history, sovereignty both spiritual and temporal. He spiritualized secular activity and to earthly hopes he gave religious sanctions.

It is remarkable that despite his tremendous and unparalleled sacrifices, like a true leader of men, he gave all the credit for his achievements to his men. The Guru never, ever claimed any privileged status for himself. Paying tribute and praising his Sikhs, he says:

The battles that I won,

I won by the grace of these people.
By their grace was I bountiful.

They were my help.

They sheltered me from harm.
Their love and generosity have
enriched my heart and home.

By their grace I acquired knowledge.

By their help I slew my foes
To serve them was I born.

They my pedestals to power
But for them I would have been
like a hundred thousand others.

The Guru had the qualities of self-discipline and moral character, in humility and service, in surrender and self-sacrifice, in catholicity of outlook, and even in the use of arms to defend one's way in life. To give a fillip to the sagging morale and to keep the spirits of his troops high, the Guru knew the value of poetry and literature. He was a scholar, poet, and polyglot; he wrote with a passion and composed poetry. Most of the literature produced by the Guru and his poets was lost during the exodus from Anandpur in the winter of 1705. That which remained was put together in one volume by Bhai Mani Singh in 1734, twenty-six years after the Guru's death. The Khalsa was made to believe that they were pure, sovereign and a chosen people. Guru Gobind's Sikhism thus became a veritable counterblast to Aurangzeb's Islam, and under his (Guru Gobind's) command the Khalsa pursued the policy of fighting fanaticism with fanaticism. In everything that the Guru wrote or spoke or did there, was a note of buoyant hope (*chardi kala*) and the conviction that even if he lost his life, his mission was bound to succeed.

Oh lord these boons of Thee I ask,
Let me never shun a righteous task,
Let me be fearless when I go to battle,
Give me faith that victory will be mine,
Give me power to sing thy praise,
And when comes the time to end my life
Let me fall in mighty strife.

- Guru Gobind Singh

In the Zafarnama (Epistle of Victory) Guru Gobind describes Aurangzeb as a deceitful fox and an irreligious man whose oaths on the Quran were not to be trusted. He also mentions: "It matters little if a jackal through cunning and treachery succeeds in killing two lion cubs, for the lion himself lives to inflict retribution on you." "I shall strike fire under the hoofs of your horses," he wrote to Aurangzeb, "and I will not let you drink the water of my Punjab." When he learnt of the death of his two younger sons and mother, he took the news with stoic calm. "What use is it to put out a few sparks when you raise a mighty flame instead?" he wrote.

Guru Gobind was a great humanist, he raised the lowest of the low (who had been in shackles for centuries) and brought them to the highest level, he made women equal in all respects to men. The Guru gave new codes of conduct; a new soldier's uniform for ease of fighting and movement and above all to be ever ready for combat and the social reforms that he introduced remain to this day the ideal of many an advanced society.

Guru Gobind's life was replete with sacrifices and suffering. It was a ceaseless struggle against injustice, oppression, tyranny, and exploitation. Here was a man who sacrificed all that he had for the cause that he espoused – his parents, four sons, a large number of followers and ultimately himself.

Dr C H Loehlin writes, *Guru Gobind was one of the most tragic figures of Indian history. In his boyhood he faced the tragedy of his father's violent death. His four sons and his mother met their death in the terrible days of the Anandpur siege and retreat. His followers were persecuted and scattered, and many of them died horrible deaths at the hands of a merciless foe.*

A London padre rightly said, *"We spread our religion (Christianity) all over the world by talking about the crucifixion of Christ, your (Sikh) history is full of thousands of Christs."* The irony is that the maximum number of people converting to Christianity and the maximum number of churches being built in India are in the state of Punjab. The people who were the first to adopt the Sikh faith and then become Khalsa are now becoming Christians. The primary reason is economic deprivation and humiliation. The fault lies with the Sikh *panth* (Sikh community regarded collectively), their *netas* (leaders and politicians), and the arrogant, land owning Sikhs.

**References:**


1. The Encyclopedia of Sikhism – Harbans Singh (Editor-in Chief)
2. Sikhism: Glimpses and Glances (Volume 1) – Bhupender Singh
3. History of the Sikhs and their Religion (Volume 1) – Edited by Kirpal Singh and Kharak Singh (published by SGPC)
4. A History of the Sikhs (Volume 1) – Khushwant Singh
5. A Short History of The Sikhs (Volume 1) – Teja Singh and Ganda Singh
6. Sikhism (Its Philosophy and History) - Edited by Daljeet Singh and Kharak Singh (published by Institute of Sikh Studies)
7. The Sikhs and their Scriptures – C H Loehlin
8. Internet (Wikipedia, the free encyclopedia)

# 8

## GURU GOBIND SINGH THE SCHOLAR AND POET

Much has been said and written about Guru Gobind Singh the warrior, but there is very little material available on the literary aspect of his life. Today, he is more popularly known as a wielder of the sword, than as a great wielder of the pen. This quality of Guru Gobind's personality that has so far remained little known to the common man must be brought to the fore and into focus. Guru possessed an inherent taste for scholarly pursuits; he was a man of letters, a great scholar, a gifted poet, and a polyglot. He knew Persian, Arabic, Sanskrit, Braj and Punjabi and, also had knowledge of the Quran.

The compositions of the Guru's works can be classified as mythological, philosophical, autobiographical, and erotic and are written in four different languages Persian, Sanskrit, Hindi, and Punjabi. At places the Guru uses all four languages in the same composition. His poetry has freshness and vigour; spiritual efficacy and the scenes of battle are recaptured in a very vivid manner. The *Bachitar Natak* is an autobiographical work and recounts the mission of his life and his *Zafarnama* (Epistle of Victory) is a letter addressed to Emperor Aurangzeb in reply to the latter's advice to surrender, after the Guru suffered military reverses and lost all his four sons.

Guru Tegh Bahadur made adequate arrangements for the education and learning of his son Gobind Rai. Bajraj Singh, a Rajput, was hired to give him military (art of warfare, swordsmanship, and handling of weapons such as lance, bow and arrow, musket, and matchlock) and equestrian training; Pir Mohammed was appointed to teach him Persian and Arabic; Bhai Gurbaksh was his Gurmukhi teacher and Pundit Harjas taught him Sanskrit and Hindi. In this way Guru Gobind Singh got all-round academic as well as military education. Bhai Kirpal Chand, maternal uncle of the Guru, was his virtual guardian during childhood.

The Guru had a rich erudite and scholarly (literary) heritage. A prolific writer, he wrote exhaustively and passionately (as he did all things), yet with such lucidity that anyone of ordinary intelligence could follow and easily understand the import of his words. He was a bright luminary on the literary horizon of the country and wrote in all the languages he had learnt, at times using all four - Persian, Sanskrit, Braj and Punjabi in the same work or writing. He rewrote parts of the Sanskrit epics in Hindi so that they could be understood by every-one. He also penned his thoughts in his autobiography: the *Bachitar Natak.*

Aurangzeb was a staunch, bigoted, and fanatic Sunni Muslim; he was a puritan and strictly followed the teaching of his religion as laid down in the Quran; he put a ban to music, singing, dancing, painting, and consumption of liquor. Since music had no place in Aurangzeb's kingdom, it is said that once the musicians took out a protest funeral procession of an effigy of music to his palace; when Aurangzeb came out, he asked them to bury the dead body of music so deep under the earth that it is never ever seen again. This is clear evidence of his hatred of fine arts.

The puritanical atmosphere of Aurangzeb's court was not conducive for creative work. The emperor shunned the arts. Painters, poets, and musicians whose traditional home had been the court in Delhi were forced to seek patronage elsewhere. Many bards and others sought Guru Gobind's patronage. Having heard of Gobind Rai's love of poetry, many poets took up their residence in his *durbar* (court). Gobind's preference of heroic verse set the tone of their compositions. They sang of brave warriors and their deeds of valour. Knowing full well the power of poetry in rousing drooping spirits, the Guru had heroic war narratives, composed by him and other poets sung by gifted bards and wedded them to martial music. This went straight to the hearts of the listeners and stirred them to high resolves for mighty deeds.

The Guru's favourite poets were Saina Pat, the author of *Gur Sobha* (one of the few reliable accounts of the Guru's life), and Nand Lal "Goya", who had pleaded the Guru's cause with Prince Muazzam. "Goya" was an accomplished scholar of Persian. Before he came to Anandpur he had held the office of the letter-writer to the prince. There is a tradition preserved among his descendants that when the King of Persia sent a dispatch to Aurangzeb, the Emperor invited his courtiers to draft a reply. Nand Lal's draft was deemed the most suitable and was selected for dispatch to Tehran. Impressed by the Hindu's learning, Aurangzeb thought it his duty to save the soul of the 'infidel' by converting him to Islam. When Nand Lal was apprised of the Emperor's intention he fled to Anandpur.

Guru Gobind knew the power of the pen and wanted his Sikhs not only to train in soldierly arts but also to cultivate letters. It is said that one day the Guru flung a handful of reed pens over the heads of the congregation, saying, "Here we will create a pool of literature. No one of my Sikhs should remain illiterate." During his stay at Paonta (1685 - 1688), on the banks of the River Yamuna, he had engaged a large number of scholars. He once asked one of those scholars employed by him, Pundit Raghunath, to teach Sanskrit to the Sikhs. The pundit refused, saying that Sanskrit was *deva bhasa* (language of the gods) and could not be taught to *Sudras* (low castes). Guru Gobind Singh selected five of the most scholarly Sikhs and sent them to Benaras (Kasi), dressed as upper-class students, to learn Sanskrit and the Hindu religious texts, to be better skilled to interpret the writings of the Gurus. These five worked diligently and on coming back as accomplished scholars began the school of Sikh theologians known as the ***Nirmalas*** (the unsullied).

After the Battle of Khidrana (Muktsar) on 29 December 1705, Guru Gobind retired for some time to the village of Talwandi Sabo. The Guru settled there and took rest and that is why the Sikhs gave the appellation *Dam Dama*, "resting or breathing place" to that location. There, along with Bhai Mani Singh, he gave final shape to the Adi Granth by incorporating the writings of his father in it. **The only writing of Guru Gobind Singh in the Guru Granth is perhaps an addition of two lines to a verse by his father on page 1429**. He also collected his own writings and put them in a separate Granth called *Dasam Granth*. From there he also sent a letter (not Zafarnama) to Aurangzeb. Apparently moved by the letter Aurangzeb issued orders that the Guru was not to be molested any further and invited Guru Gobind to meet him. It was because of the literary activities of the Guru that Talwandi Sabo earned the title of '*Guru Ki Kasi*' or Guru's Benaras.

## DASAM GRANTH

THE COLLECTION of writings attributed to Guru Gobind Singh is known as the *Dasam Granth* or *Dasam Padshah ka Granth*. It consists of the following eighteen works:

*Jap Sahib, Akal Ustat, Bachitar Natak, Chandi Charitr I, Chandi Charitr II, Chandi di Var, Gyan Parbodh, Chaubis Avatar, Mehdi Mir Budh, Brahma Avatar, Rudra Avatar, Sabad Hazare, Sri Mukh bak Swaiye, Khalsa di Mehima, Sastra Nam Mala, Pakhyan Caritr, Zafarnama and the Hikayats.* These works are written in four different languages Braj (frequently highly Sanskritized), Hindi, Persian and Gurmukhi.

The compositions can be classified as mythological, philosophical, autobiographical and erotic. The largest portion of the compilation is mythological, relating well known tales of Hindu mythology. The *Chandi Charitr* and *Mehdi Mir Budh, Brahma Avatar* and *Rudra Avatar* are similar tales of reincarnation of different aspects of the Hindu trinity.

The Jap Sahib (distinct from Guru Nanak's Japji) and *Akal Ustat, Gyan Parbodh, Sabad Hazare,* and some hymns are philosophical and devotional and are used in Sikh ritual prayer.

Most of the works mention the date and place of composition and help to fix the movements of the Guru. *Bachitar Natak* is autobiographical and recounts the mission of the Guru. In the same category though in a different context, is the *Zafarnama* (Epistle of Victory) which the Guru, after having suffered military reverses and having lost all his four sons, addressed to Emperor Aurangzeb in reply to the latter's advice to surrender.

The *Pakhyan Caritr* and the *Hikayats* are tales of the wiles of women in a corrupt society.

**Date of Compilation**

Most of the *Dasam Granth* was compiled in Anandpur. The Guru recompiled the writings of his predecessors as well as reproduced some portions of the *Dasam Granth* during his sojourn in the village of Damdama.

**Present versions of the Dasam Granth**

The task of reproducing the works of Guru Gobind was undertaken after his death by his companion and disciple, Bhai Mani Singh, who spent nine years at the task. He was able to get some copies from other disciples and filled in the gaps from memory.

There are many compilations in existence today, and more are being discovered. The one written by Bhai Mani Singh in his own hand is in the possession of Gulab Singh Sethi of New Delhi and the volumes at the Gurdwaras in Patna and Sangrur are the three better known compilations.

**Authenticity of Writings of the Dasam Granth**

Scholars differ in their views on the subject. Dr D P Astha, Dr Trilochan Singh, and Dr Mohan Singh are among those who hold that all the writing ascribed to Guru Gobind Singh was in fact the Guru's work. But Messrs Macauliffe, Cunningham, Narang and Banerjee do not believe that all the writing in the *Dasam Granth* is that of Guru Gobind Singh. The controversy arises from the fact that during his ministry, Guru Gobind was too busy reforming his church, and defending himself and his disciples against the frequent attacks from his enemies, to be able to devote much time to composition. Secondly it is difficult to distinguish the works of the Guru from the compositions of the fifty-two bards in his employ. Thus, the only portions which can be ascribed with some certainty to him are those which by his sanction became a part of Sikh ritual and prayer, and his autobiography. Such are the *Jap Sahib, Akal Ustat, Gyan Parbodh, Sabad Hazare,* the *Chaupayis*, the *Bachitar Natak* and the *Zafarnama.* The scribes in his court must have copied these compositions soon after the Guru composed them at Anandpur. They were then distributed to Sikh communities so that they could be incorporated in daily prayer and religious functions. The Guru may have had a hand in the composition of some of the others, but any categorical assertion on the subject would be hazardous.

**Language and literary Quality**

The language of most of the *Dasam Granth* is largely Braj, veering towards Sanskrit at one extreme and simple colloquial Hindi at the other. The *Zafarnama and Hikayats* are in Persian; several passages in other works are in Punjabi. Often new words are coined: half Arabic and half Sanskrit (and sometimes words without meaning just to create musical effect).

The descriptions of scenes of battle are couched in extreme vigorous staccato rhyme often reduced to lines of one word each. The battles waged by Chandi and the Guru's encounters with the hill chiefs at Bhangani and Nadaun are the most stirring that exist.

Guru Gobind Singh loved nature and often spent hours in solitude on the banks of River Yamuna. It was there that he was inspired to write poetry. The scenes of nature and love, particularly in the *Krishana Avatar*, are haunting in their loveliness:

> Besides the sparkling waters of the river,
> On the banks in silver moonlight bathed
> Were strewn jasmine petals as if to make a bed
> And blossoms turned over head to make a bower.
> Krishna took Radha by the hand, tilted up her face
> And gazed upon her beauty. Then clasped
> The damsel fair in his dark arms
> As a black shape eclipses the moon.
> Spake Krishna: "Maiden fair, I sent not for thee.
> I am as a deer wounded by the hunter's dart.
> Thy love-lorn eyes have pierced my heart.
> Beloved mine! Thy wraths burn fire

Hath singed my limbs but I wished not to depart.
I came not at thy command, but to soothe
My burns before the warmth of thy love ".

Krishna Avtar

**Translations of four small selections from the Dasam Granth**

(a) *Bachitar Natak*:

For though my thoughts were lost in prayer
At the feet of almighty God,
I was ordained to establish a sect and lay down its rules.
But whosoever regards me as Lord
Shall be damned and destroyed.
I am - and of this let there be no doubt -
I am but the slave of God as other men are,
A beholder of the wonders of creation.

(b) *Jap Sahib* :

*Chakra cehan ar baru jat ar pat nahinjal.*

God has no marks or symbols
He is of no colour, of no caste,
He is not even of any lineage.
His form, hue, shape and garb
Cannot be described by anyone.
He is immovable; He is self-existent;
He shines out in his own splendor;
There is no one who can measure His might.
He is the King of Kings, the lordly Indra
Of countless Indras, the Supreme Sovereign
Of the three worlds of gods, men, and demons;
Nay, even the meadows and woodlands
Cry in praise of Him: "Infinite, Infinite!"
O Lord who can tell the count of Thy names?
According to Thy deeds will I
Endeavour to relate Thy names.

(c) *Swaiye*:

Some worship stones and on their heads bear them,
Some the phallus strung as necklaces wear its emblem.
Some behold their God in the south, some to the west bow their head.
Some worship images, others are busy praying to the dead.
The world is bound in false ritual
And God's secret is still unread.

(d) *Sabad Hazare*:

If you want to practice asceticism, do it in this way:
Let thine own house be the forest
Thy heart the anchorite
Eat little, sleep little,
Learn to love, be merciful and forbear.
Be mild, be patient,
Have no lust, nor wrath,
Greed nor obstinacy.

A lot of quality literary work was produced by Guru Gobind Singh and the bards under his patronage at Anandpur, Paonta and Talwandi Sabo (*Dam Dama* or *Guru Ki Kasi*). Most of the literature created by the Guru and his poets was lost during the exodus from Anandpur in the winter of 1705. That which remained was put together in one volume by Bhai Mani Singh in 1734, twenty-six years after the Guru's death. From the literature that has trickled down to us after all the vagaries of the turbulent times, turmoil of the fiercely fought battles and trials and tribulations in the life of the Guru and the Khalsa, we find that Guru Gobind Singh was not only a great warrior and fearless soldier but also a man of eminent learning, an admirable philosopher, a distinguished scholar and an adept intellectual.

**Note**: After leaving Anandpur, following the Sixth Battle of Anandpur, with the enemy in hot pursuit, a huge amount of Guru Gobind's work (religious and literary wealth) along with valuable property and equipment was drowned while crossing the Sarsa River, which was in spate.

**References:**

1. The Encyclopedia of Sikhism – Harbans Singh (Editor-in Chief)
2. Sikhism: Glimpses and Glances (Volume 1) – Bhupender Singh
3. History of the Sikhs and their Religion (Volume 1) – Edited by Kirpal Singh and Kharak Singh (published by SGPC)
4. A History of the Sikhs (Volume 1) – Khushwant Singh
5. Homage to Guru Gobind Singh - Khushwant Singh and Suneet Vir Singh
6. Guru Gobind Singh – Gopal Singh
7. The Sikhs and their Scriptures – C H Loehlin

# 9

# THREE ORDERS ESTABLISHED BY GURU GOBIND SINGH

We may classify these as orders since they differ mainly in their function and practices rather than in their fundamental beliefs from mainstream Sikhism. All have the Adi Granth as their Scripture and acknowledge the ten gurus.

## THE NIHANG OR AKALI SIKHS

The Nihangs are a militant order among the Sikh people. The word Nihang is from the Persian *nihang* meaning crocodile, alligator, shark, or water dragon, and signifies qualities of ferocity and fearlessness. They are also known as the reckless ones, though some say the word means naked. The word Nihang and Akali are synonymous. The term Akali means immortal, and the order is so called because they are worshippers of the Immortal One or God Almighty. Nihangs or Akalis (servitors of the timeless God), wear blue and dedicate their lives to the service of the community. The Akalis are the only aggressive, not to say fanatical core of the Khalsa fraternity. Guru Gobind Singh himself founded and organized this sect as a counterpoise to the Pathan Ghazi.

These dedicated soldiers of the Khalsa – "immortals" as they genuinely believed themselves to be – devoted themselves to the care of Sikh shrines and it was their sacred duty to protect the society at that particular period of time. They were humble and pious people continually praying and doing menial jobs for the love of the Guru in holy places and gurdwaras; they had an extreme sense of devotion and dedication to their cause and few personal needs. The blind fidelity to their Gurus made them place their properties and even lives at their disposal. The Akalis were fanatics and to serve a temporal or foreign master was against their creed and tenets.

Their best quality was their dashing gallantry, and they were equally adept and apt to fighting on foot as well as on horseback. These men were tall and hardy, excellent warriors and capable of moving at great speed and of enduring hardships that could decimate an army on foot. Their equestrian skills were superb and even today they keep horses in their *deras* (camps/habitation), and their horsemanship is admirable.

These men knew no fear. The Nihangs had won a name for valour and believed that they were invincible. They were, always under arms, the berserks of the clan who went to battle as if they were going to a feast. They were dour and disciplined fighters, full of fire and dog like in their devotion to their religion and Gurus. They had fierce and uncontrolled passions and their temper was hot and imperious; they were savage, wild, fierce, and tenacious with a lust for battle and made brutal attacks. They were the flower of the Sikh armies. Whenever there was an especially dangerous or bloody task to be done or any difficulty or hurdle to be overcome, requiring courage and fearlessness to a very high degree, the Akalis were usually chosen to perform it. These people were an answer to the Muslim Ghazis and the enemy dreaded them.

They enjoyed a good deal of popularity among the Sikh masses. In the matter of religious doctrine and practice, they were uncompromisingly orthodox. According to Ali-ud-Din Mufti, the Akalis were an order that never cared about death and misery. And because of the respect for this order the Sikhs were strictly forbidden from oppressing these people or shedding their blood and doing so was a sinful act. The Akalis have, ever since their origin, been held in high esteem by the Sikhs. Their contingents were called the forces of Guru Gobind Singh. Therefore, they enjoyed the regard of the whole Sikh community. It was for this reason that the Shahid or Nihang Misl was held in deep veneration.

The Nihangs have a glorious past and during their heydays they were admired, respected, and held in high esteem. Maharaja Ranjit Singh gave the Nihangs a lot of concessions, perks, and privileges, but they refused to take any pay/remuneration for their services. They were venerated, honoured and recognized for their daring deeds, chivalry and dauntless courage, but since the annexation of the Punjab the sect is declining.

**The Nihangs are still living in the past; they live in a world of their own, of past memory, not divorced from fancy; their dress and lifestyle have not changed much. They live as they lived 300 years ago, in the same mould and in a time warp – same type of clothing, same type of weapons and attitude and they still maintain and ride horses. Even today, they are accomplished horsemen. You can watch the Nihangs during the Holla Mohalla festival – displaying their equestrian and martial skills and, people come from all over the world to watch them and shoot them with their cameras.**

**In present times, the order has degenerated to a laughingstock. They are rigid adherents to the five K's prescribed by Guru Gobind Singh, but to show their absolute devotion to the sword, they supplement the 5 K's by carrying steel about their person to a very ridiculous extent. Nevertheless, they are a picturesque lot – the Sikh version of the Spanish author Miguel de Cervantes' Don Quixote with speech full of braggadocio.**

- The Nihangs and Akalis were identical till the middle of the nineteenth century, when the Sikh political supremacy was extinguished in Punjab. Akali, a term now appropriated by members of the dominant Sikh political party, the Shiromani Akali Dal, founded on 14 December 1920 was earlier used for Nihangs (q.v.), an order of armed religious zealots among the baptized Sikhs (Khalsa). The Akali Dal launched the Gurdwara Reform Movement (a.k.a. Akali movement) in 1922. This was when the Akalis and Nihangs really began to be considered as separate entities.

## NIRMALA SIKHS

**Nirmalas**, derived from the Sanskrit *nirmala* meaning spotless, unsullied, pure, bright, etc. is the name of an order of Sikhs engaged in religious study and preaching. The order came into being during the time of Guru Gobind Singh (1666-1708), though some, on the authority of a line in the first *var* of Bhai Gurdas (d. 1636), claim like the *Udasis*, Guru Nanak (1469-1539) himself to be the founder.

Guru Gobind wanted his followers not only to acquire skills in warfare but also to cultivate letters. He once asked one of the scholars employed by him, Pundit Raghunath, to teach Sanskrit to the Sikhs. He refused, saying that Sanskrit was *deva bhasa* (language of the gods) and could not be taught to *Sudras* (low castes). Guru Gobind Singh selected five of the most scholarly Sikhs, namely, Karam Singh, Vir Singh, Ganda Singh, Saina Singh and Ram Singh and sent them to Benaras (Varanasi, the centre of Hindu learning), dressed as upper-class students to learn Sanskrit and the Hindu religious texts, to be better able to interpret the writings of the Gurus. These Sikhs worked diligently for several years and returned to Anandpur as accomplished scholars of classical Indian theology and philosophy. These five began the school of Sikh theologians known as the ***nirmalas*** (the unsullied). In view of their piety and sophisticated manner, they and their students came to be known as Nirmalas and were later recognised as a separate order. The order has several sub-orders each with its own dera (camp/habitation) and following.

The Nirmalas believe in the ten Gurus and Guru Granth Sahib. They generally do not take the Khalsa baptism, don ochre-coloured garments, mostly practice celibacy and are devoted to scriptural and philosophical studies. By tradition they are inclined towards classical Hindu philosophy especially Vedanta. They have mastery over the Sanskrit language and the Vedas. They also take out their own *raths* (carriage pulled by horses) during the *kumbh Melas*.

Their contribution towards the preaching of Sikh doctrine and production of philosophical literature in Sanskrit, Braj, Hindi and Punjabi is considerable. All sacred Hindu texts and a number of other Hindu classics have been translated and a vast number of books in various languages have also been written by them. The headquarters of the Nirmala sect is in Kankhal. They have *Akharas* (monastery/seminary) in all major Hindu centers – Kankhal, Haridwar, Rishikesh, Benaras (Varanasi or Kashi), Allahabad (Prayag), Ujjain, Gaya, Triyambak (Nasik), Patna, Kurukshetra and in Punjab.

The Nirmala saints have done yeoman service to the Sikh *panth* (community) in the literary field and also in preaching, conserving, and preserving Sikh annals, manuscripts, and scriptures, culture and institutions, especially, during the turbulent period of persecution of the Sikhs, when the Khalsa was being hunted and were gentlemen at large, living off the land and hiding in remote places.

Now famous as the *Eco Baba,* **Baba Balbir Singh Seechewal** (born 2 February 1962) is a Nirmala Sikh. He single handedly cleaned and restored Kali Bein River, a 160 km long tributary of Beas in Doaba region of Punjab. He says, "It is said in the Bani (Guru's gospel) that it is better to save a creature, than to take bath in 68 holy places of pilgrimage." He was awarded with the Padmashri by the Government of India (2017) and Hero of Environment by TIME magazine.

## SEWA PANTHI SIKHS

During the Battle of Anandpur (1705), **Bhai Kanhaiya** (1648-1718*),* happened to be visiting Anandpur. He went around the battlefield serving water to the wounded and dying, every day, without distinction of friend or foe. Some Sikhs complained about him to Guru Gobind Singh. On being questioned, he replied that he saw no Sikhs or Mughals, but the Guru's face in everyone. The Guru was pleased and praised him for his deep understanding of the Sikh doctrines. After blessing Bhai Kanhaiya, Guru Gobind Singh, told him that he had profoundly comprehended the teachings of Sikhism and should keep on serving humanity to the best of his ability as long as he could.

After the Battle of Anandpur, Bhai Kanhaiya retired to his native place (Sodhara) and established a *dharamshala* at Kavha village (Attock district, now in Pakistan), which he turned into a preaching centre. He founded the **Sewapanthi order**, and his special mission was selfless service to humanity at large with no discriminion whatsoever. Though Bhai Kanhaiya founded the Sewapanthi order, the actual idea, inspiration, motivation, and primary driving force behind the order was Guru Gobind Singh.

Bhai Sewa Ram led the Sewapanthi order after the death of its founder Bhai Kanhaiya (1718), a disciple of Guru Gobind Singh. Addan Shahis is another name for the Sewapanthi order, derived from Addan Shah, a renowned Sewapanthi saint.

Although, Sewapanthis are counted as a sect among the Sikhs, they depart in certain respects from the Sikh way of life: a Sewapanthi saint, for instance, lives the life of a recluse, renouncing all worldly attachments and remains a celibate. Humility, service, generosity, detachment and contentment are the common virtues recommended. Yet contrary to Sikh principle, there is an emphasis on celibacy. The Sewapanthis include both Khalsa and *Sahaj Dhari* (those who would take time to adopt the Five K's) Sikhs.

The Sewapanthi tradition flourished in southwest Punjab for nearly 12 generations until 1947. This sect (variously known as Sewapanthis, Sewa Dassiey, and Addan Shahis), is best symbolized by Bhai Kanhaiya who, though himself a Sikh, aided wounded Sikh and Muslim soldiers alike during the Tenth Sikh Guru's wars with the Moghuls. They wore distinctive white robes.

Sewapanthis introduced a new dimension to the sub continental religious philosophies. They believed that sewa (helping the needy) was the highest form of spiritual meditation - higher than singing hymns or reciting holy books. The creation of Pakistan dealt a devastating blow to the Sewapanthis and they never got truly transplanted in the new "East" Punjab. They are extinct today and it has been an irreparable loss to humanity. An extremely valuable asset was lost for posterity.

Quite in contrast to the militant Nihangs are Nirmala (devoted to literary pursuits) and Sewapanthi (devoted to doing service/*sewa* to humanity) *sants* or saints. One cannot help but admire the farsightedness and wide range of interests of the tenth guru in sponsoring the rise of three such widely different orders as the Nihangs, Nirmalas and Sewapanthis; yet for the all-round development of the Khalsa each was needed to supplement the others.

**References:**


1. The Encyclopedia of Sikhism – Harbans Singh (Editor-in Chief)
2. Sikhism: Glimpses and Glances (Volume 1 and 2) – Bhupender Singh
3. History of the Sikhs and their Religion (Volume 1) – Edited by Kirpal Singh and Kharak Singh (published by SGPC)
4. A History of the Sikhs (Volume 1) – Khushwant Singh
5. The Sikhs and their Scriptures – C H Loehlin

# 10

## GURU GOBIND SINGH'S MUSLIM FRIENDS AND ADMIRERS

Guru Gobind Singh was never against Islam, or for that matter, against any religion. He said, "The temple and the mosque are the same; the Hindu worship and the Musalman prayer are the same; Allah and Abhekh (unknowable) are the same; Puranas and Quran are the same. They are all alike; it is One God who created all." He continued to have Muslim friends and attendants and did not ever allow his movement to become anti-Islamic, although his father, the ninth Guru, Tegh Bahadur (1621-1675) had been executed by the order of Aurangzeb in 1675. And, also despite the fact, that two of his sons died fighting the Mughals and the remaining two were executed by the orders of the Muslim Governor of Sirhind. He paid the price for this when he was murdered in October 1708 by two Muslims.

In the battle of Anandpur Sahib, in 1704, when some Sikhs complained against Bhai Kanhaiya for serving water to wounded soldiers, including those belonging to the enemy camp, the Guru called him and said that it was people like Kanhaiya who had imbibed the real spirit of Sikhism. Those historians, who think that Guru Gobind Singh was anti–Islam, have not studied his life and writings with an open mind. There is not a word in his speeches or writings against Muslims or Islam. He was against religious oppression of the cruel Mughal government. He was an embodiment of love for all and believed in equality and brotherhood of mankind. For him, the temple and mosque were the same.

A list of Guru Gobind's Muslim friends and admirers is appended.

**Pir Bhikhan Shah** or **Shah Bhikh Pir** was a seventeenth - century Sufi saint and a disciple of Abul Mu'ali Shah (a Sufi divine of Ambhita, near Saharanpur – UP). Soon, he became a *pir* (a Sufi Muslim saint or holy man) of much repute and piety in his own right. He was son of Sayyid

Muhammad Yusaf of Siana Sayyidan, a village 5 km from Pehova (Kurukshetra district – Haryana). For some time, he lived in Ghuram (near Patiala) and finally settled in Thaska (Kurukshetra district).

According to *Sri Gur Prartap Suraj Granth* by Bhai Santokh Singh, one day, Pir Bhikhan Shah genuflected towards the east rather than the Kaaba in the west. On being asked about the sacrilege, the Pir answered that a divine messiah had taken birth in a city in the east. Pir Bhikhan Shah, with his disciples travelled all the way to Patna to have a glimpse of the infant child, Guru Gobind Singh. Desiring to know what the attitude of the Guru would be towards the two major religious people of the country, he placed two small pots in front of the child. The baby reached out and simultaneously covered both pots with his tiny hands. The Pir felt happy that the new seer would treat Hindus and Muslims alike and show equal respect to both. Sikh chronicles record another meeting between the two at Lakhnaur, near Ambala in 1672, where the Guru was on a sojourn on his way from Patna to Kiratpur.

**Nawab Rahim Baksh and Nawab Karim Baksh** were among the famous Muslim admirers of the Tenth Master. A village and two gardens gifted by the two brothers to the Guru when he was a baby are still attached to Gurdwara Patna Sahib.

**Pir Buddhu Shah** (1647 – 1704), a Muslim divine whose real name was Badr ud-Din. He was an admirer of Guru Gobind Singh. Because of his simplicity and quiet nature during childhood, he was given the nickname Buddhu (literally simpleton). In 1685, at Paonta, on his recommendation the Guru engaged 500 Pathan soldiers under the command of four leaders, Kale Khan, Bhikhan Khan, Nijabat Khan and Hayat Khan. In 1686, when Guru Gobind Singh was attacked by a combined force of the hill chiefs led by Raja Fateh Shah of Srinagar (Garhwal), all the Pathans except for Kale Khan deserted him and joined hands with the hill monarch. The news of the treachery was sent to the Pir. He immediately rushed to the battlefield of Bhangani, with his brother, four sons and 700 of his followers. The battle was won, but at a very heavy cost. Pir

Buddhu Shah lost his brother Bhure Shah, two sons Ashraf and Muhammad Shah and many of his disciples.

The rich presents offered to the Pir after the battle by Guru Gobind Singh were politely declined by him. He however requested the Guru for the *kangha* (comb) stuck in his hair and the turban that he was about to tie. Guru Gobind Singh granted his wish and gave him the two articles along with a small *kirpan*. The Pir and his descendants kept these items in their family as sacred heirlooms until Maharaja Bharpur Singh of Nabha (1840-63) acquired them in exchange for a *jagir* (land grant).

Complaints about the Pir regarding the assistance that he had rendered to Guru Gobind Singh reached the imperial government at Delhi. The *faujdar* (army commander) of Sirhind ordered Usman Khan to deal with Pir Buddhu Shah. The Pir was arrested at Sadhaura (Ambala district), his hometown and executed on 21 March 1704. The great Sikh General Banda Singh Bahadur avenged the Pir's execution in 1709 by storming Sadhaura and killing Usman Khan. Pir Buddhu Shah's descendants migrated to Pakistan in 1947. Their ancestral house in Sadhaura has been converted into a Gurdwara named after Pir Buddhu Shah. It will also be worth mentioning here that a *palang* (bed) gifted to Guru Gobind Singh by Pir Buddhu Shah is placed in the Singh Sabha Gurdwara at Jodhpur.

**Nihang Khan**, the Muslim chief of Kotla Nihang Khan, near Ropar, in Punjab, was a devotee of Guru Gobind Singh. According to Sarup Singh Kaushish, *Guru kian Sakhian*, he with his wife and sons attended Baisakhi festival at Anandpur in 1694 and rendered homage to the Guru. At his request, Guru Gobind Singh visited him in his village a month later, on the occasion of the betrothal of his son and blessed the family. After the evacuation of Anandpur (December 1705), the Guru came to Nihang Khan and left the same night. The Guru's two elder sons and forty Sikhs had accompanied him. Nihang Khan detailed his son, Alam Khan, to guide them on the route they were to follow.

**Mumtaz**. According to *Guru kian Sakhian* by Sarup Singh Kaushish, Mumtaz was the daughter of Nihang Khan, the Muslim chief of Kotla

Nihang Khan, near Ropar. She nursed and looked after the Sikh warrior and martyr, Bhai Bachittar Singh who was mortally wounded in a skirmish after the evacuation of Anandpur in December 1705. He was carried to the house of Nihang Khan by Sahibzada Ajit Singh in a serious condition. In order to conceal the seriously injured soldier and evade the enemy pursuers, Nihang Khan told them that the grievously wounded man in the house was his son-in-law. Even Mumtaz declared Bhai Bachittar Singh to be her husband. The latter, though well looked after by his hosts succumbed to his injuries. Mumtaz, though engaged to a suitable young man from her community, refused to get married and dedicated the rest of her life to the Guru and his principles.

**Nabi Khan** and **Ghani Khan**, the cousins of Nihang Khan (History of Sikhs and their Religion published by SGPC - page 302) were horse dealers of Machiwara in present day Ludhiana district of Punjab. The Guru had known them earlier for they had visited the Guru at Anandpur and sold a number of good horses to him. They saved the Guru's life. After the Battle of Chamkaur (1705) when the Guru reached Machiwara, the two Pathan brothers carried Guru Gobind in a curtained palanquin in the guise of *Uchch da Pir* (Sufi Muslim saint of Uchch) and helped him get past the Mughal sentries and make good his escape to the Malwa region. They escorted him till Hehran, a village near Raikot in Ludhiana. The Guru gave them an autographed letter of commendation and his blessings. The letter was reverently preserved by their descendants. The family migrated to Pakistan in 1947. Their house in Machiwara is now Gurdwara Uchch da Pir.

**Quazi Pir Mohammad** had been the Persian tutor of Guru Gobind Singh and the Guru's proficiency in Persian is evident from his works especially Zafarnama (Epistle of Victory) written to Aurangzeb. While being carried in the guise of *Uchch da Pir* by the two Pathan brothers; the party was overtaken by a pursuing enemy contingent. On interrogating the escort about the identity of the *Pir*, the commander finding the answers, not very satisfactory sent for Quazi Pir Mohammad. The Quazi recognized the Guru but he did not give him away. On receiving a satisfactory reply from Quazi Pir Mohammad, the commander let the party proceed. The families of these Mohammedan friends still retain the autographed letters granted to them by the Guru and show them with great respect to those who visit their houses.

**Begum Zaina** was the wife of the notorious Wazir Khan (d 1710), Nawab of Sirhind. She tried her best to dissuade her husband from being cruel and unjust to the two younger sons (Zorawar Singh and Fateh Singh, aged nine and seven years respectively) of Guru Gobind Singh. But when he did not relent and had them murdered, she committed suicide by stabbing herself.

**Rai Kallah** was the chief of Raikot; an erstwhile state (near Ludhiana) comprising 1360 villages, founded by Rai Ahmed in 1648. According to History of Sikhs and their Religion published by SGPC – page 302; Rai Kallah's daughter was married to Alam Khan, the son of Nihang Khan. He gave shelter to Guru Gobind when he was on the run after the battle of Chamkaur in 1705. He risked not just his own life but that of his family and subjects and even the peril of losing his property and entire state by incurring the wrath of Aurangzeb, the emperor.

On Guru Gobind's request, Rai Kallah sent his servant, Nura Mahi (his sister was married at Sirhind) to Sirhind and procured news about the Guru's two younger sons and old mother. The Guru stayed with Rai Kallah for three days and left on the fourth day; while departing he gave three items *Ganga Sagar* (a copper kettle with 288 holes), a *Rehal* (small lectern or folding wooden stool to support a book while reading in the sitting position - popular in oriental countries) and *Sri Sahib* (an excellent and expensive small sword) to the family. All that remains today is the *Ganga Sagar*, since the sword was taken away by the British in the 19th century and the *rehal*, being wooden, could not withstand the vagaries of nature for over 300 years. The family migrated to Pakistan in 1947.

The name of Rai Kallah, figures prominently in Sikh history and chronicles. Rai Azizullah the 9th descendent of the Rai family after Rai Kalha keeps the Ganga Sagar (a very important and invaluable gift and heirloom of the family) in a special bank vault in Canada. Gurdwara Sri Tahliana Sahib is the main Gurdwara in the town of Raikot. Guru Gobind Singh arrived in the evening and rested under a *Tahli* or *Sheesham* tree (Punjab Teak), hence the name of the Gurdwara.

**Sher Mohammad Khan, the Nawab of Malerkotla**. The Nawabs of Malerkotla (a Muslim city some 20 miles south of Ludhiana) were Sherwani Afghans who, in turn were descendants of Sheikh Sarduddin. The Sheikh had been gifted sixty-eight villages near Ludhiana in East-Punjab when he married the daughter of Sultan Bahlol Lodhi.

When Guru Gobind came to know that none except the Nawab of Malerkotla, had pleaded the case of his two small sons, who were bricked alive on the orders of the Nawab of Sirhind, he is known to have remarked that the roots of the oppressive Mughals would be dug up but the roots of Malerkotla would remain forever green. The Sikhs have always remembered this protest of the Nawab with gratitude, and throughout their relations with the Muslim powers they have always spared the house of Malerkotla from their attacks. The Sikhs never molested Malerkotla even when the whole surrounding country was devastated after the Battle of Sirhind by Banda Bahadur. The Muslim population in Malerkotla was not touched in the rioting, during the partition of the country. The present Nawab of Malerkotla still possesses the sword presented by the Guru to his ancestors.

**Maimun Khan, Sayyed Beg (d. 1703) and Said Khan**. Maimun Khan, a Mughal commander, joined Guru Gobind Singh in response to the call of his conscience. He commanded a troop of 100 Afghan soldiers in the service of the Guru. Sayyed Beg, another Mughal commander, was won over by the Guru's magnetic personality; he deserted his post and fought for the Guru as he thought it unjust to fight against the Guru.

During the fifth Battle of Anandpur (February 1703), Guru Gobind was attacked by a large Mugal army from Lahore, under General Said Khan. Guru Gobind Singh had only 500 warriors with him, at that time. A fierce battle ensued, in which Maimun Khan with his 100 Muslim retainers and Sayyed Beg fought on the Guru's side with conspicuous courage. **In this battle Sayyed Beg fell fighting for the Guru**. Guru Gobind Singh came face to face with Said Khan and challenged him. Said Khan had heard stories about the Guru and for long, he had cherished a desire to meet him. On seeing Guru Gobind, he was won over by his charismatic personality. He threw away his sword, deserted his post and vowed never to use it against the Sikhs again. Dismounting his horse, he touched the Guru's stirrup to do homage to him. Guru Gobind Singh blessed him, and he quietly left the battlefield. He became a recluse and spent the rest of his life in prayer. Said Khan's sister, a pious lady, Nasiran was married to Pir Buddhu Shah, when he (the *pir*) was 18 years of age.

**The Three Fakirs - Arif Din, Ghias-ud-Din, and Ibrahim.** These three holy men were devotees and admirers of Guru Gobind. Pir Arif Din, a famous Fakir of Lakhnaur saw the child Guru at play when he was driving past him. He got down from his carriage and humbly bowed before him. He told his enraged followes that he had just offered salaam to Allah the Great. "Brother Fakir Ghias-ud-Din whom do you belong to?" asked Guru Gobind. The Fakir pointed to his friend, philosopher, and guide Bhai Nand Lal. Before his devoted disciples could correct him, Guru Gobind replied that since Bhai Nand Lal belonged to him, they both belonged to him. Such was the large heartedness of the Guru. Fakir Ibrahim, who had a large following met the Guru in the Lakhi Jungle and became his devoted follower.

**Bahadur Shah**. In 1696 Emperor Aurangzeb (1618 – 20 February 1707) sent his son Prince Muazzam later **Emperor Bahadur Shah** (1643 – 1712) to chastise Guru Gobind Singh. The prince himself stationed himself at Lahore and sent Mirza Beg to deal with the Guru and the hill chiefs. The latter were severely punished, but the Guru was left alone. This was due to the intercession of Bhai Nand Lal, who was a devout *Sahaj Dhari* Sikh and a *Diwan* or secretary to the Prince. Bhai Nand Lal seems to have brought about some sort of an understanding between the Prince and the Guru. The former became a friend and admirer of the latter. Later the Guru assisted Bahadur Shah in the war of succession by sending a detachment of his trusted Sikhs to fight in the Battle of Jaju near Agra on 08 June 1707. After Bahadur Shah became emperor, he invited Guru Gobind to Agra, treated him with utmost respect, and presented him with a rich dress of honour and a jeweled scarf (*dhukhdhukhi*) worth sixty thousand rupees. Towards the end of his life even Aurangzeb repented and invited the Guru to meet him.

The secret behind all this is that Guru Gobind Singh was an embodiment of love and a great humanitarian who propagated true love without distinction of caste, creed, and faith. Such was the devotion that the Guru enjoyed from his devotees of all faiths.

**References:**


1. The Encyclopedia of Sikhism – Harbans Singh (Editor-in Chief)
2. Sikhism: Glimpses and Glances – Bhupender Singh
3. History of the Sikhs and their Religion (Volume 1) – Edited by Kirpal Singh and Kharak Singh (published by SGPC)
4. A Short History of The Sikhs (Volume 1) – Teja Singh and Ganda Singh
5. A History of the Sikhs (Volume 1) – Khushwant Singh
6. Abstracts of Sikh Studies - January-March 2017 issue
7. The Sikhs and their Scriptures – C H Loehlin
8. Glimpses of The Sikh Gurus (For Children) – Mukhtar S Goraya

# 11

# FIFTEEN PROMINENT SIKHS OF GURU GOBIND SINGH'S PERIOD

Although, a lot is said and written about leaders and generals and their deeds and exploits, it is the rank and file (the common man) that helped, fought, and died for the leader in accomplishing his task and mission that are forgotten over a period of time. The ravages of time, engulfs everything in the depths of obscurity. Against the flow of time History is a robust rampart. All happenings that History intercepts survive and are preserved for posterity. History does not let them pass away into the abysses of oblivion.

This article or chapter is a sine qua non in order to remember and keep alive the memory of these forgotten, and unsung fiery warriors of Guru Gobind Singh, who laid down their lives fighting against the evil and tyrannical forces that were determined to convert the whole country into an Islamic state. It is a tribute to their sacrifice, dedication, devotion, and courage of conviction. It has been rightly said that Nations that are unaware of their history and cultures are gradually erased from the globe.

**Panj Payare (Five Beloved Ones)**

**1. Bhai Daya Singh** (1661-1708), was one of the *Panj Payare* (Five Beloved Ones) i.e., the first five Sikhs, of tested courage and loyalty, who initially came into the fold of the Khalsa, and constituted the nucleus of the new order (the Khalsa). He was the son of Bhai Suddha, a Sobti Khatri of Lahore and Mai Diali. His father, Bhai Suddha was a devout Sikh of Guru Tegh Bahadur, who had permanently settled down with his family at Anandpur in 1677. In the historic gathering in Keshgarh Fort at Anandpur, on 29 March 1699, Daya Ram was the first Sikh to rise to offer his head at the Guru's call and after initiation became Daya Singh from Daya Ram (his original name). He took part in the battles of Anandpur and was one of the three Sikhs who followed Guru Gobind Singh out of Chamkaur on the night of 7/8 December 1705, eluding the enemy. He, along with Bhai Dharam Singh, was the Guru's emissary sent to deliver his letter, *Zafarnamah* (Epistle of Victory), to Emperor Aurangzeb, at Ahmadnagar. A shrine called Gurdwara Bhai Daya Singh marks the place of his sojourn in Dhami Mahalla. Bhai Daya Singh remained in attendance upon the Guru and was with him at the time of his death at Nanded on 07 October 1708. Daya Singh died at Nanded, soon after the Guru's death and a joint memorial for him and his companion Bhai Dharam Singh known as Angitha (lit. burning pyre) Bhai Daya Singh *ate* (and) Bhai Dharam Singh, marks the site of their cremation.

Bhai Daya Singh was a learned man. One of the Rahitnamas (manuals on Sikh conduct), is ascribed to him. The Nirmalas, a sect of Sikhs, claim him as one of their forebears. Their Darauli branch traces its origin to Bhai Daya Singh through Baba Deep Singh.

**2. Bhai Dharam Singh** (1666-1708), was the son of a farmer (*Jat*), Bhai Sant Ram and Mai Sabho, of Hastinapur, an ancient town on the right bank of the Ganges, 35 km north-east of Meerut. On the historic Baisakhi congregation (29 March 1699), at Anandpur, Dharam Das happened to be in the crowd. He responded to one of the five calls by Guru Gobind Singh and offered to lay down his head for the Guru. Thus, he became one of the *Panj Payare* (Five Beloved Ones) and became Dharam Singh from Dharam Das. He took part in the battles of Anandpur and was in Guru Gobind's train when Anandpur and thereafter Chamkaur were evacuated. Dharam Singh accompanied Bhai Daya Singh to deliver Guru Gobind Singh's letter, the *Zafarnamah*, to Emperor Aurangzeb.

After the death of Aurangzeb (20 February 1707), Bhai Dharam Singh fought in the battle of Jajau (08 June 1707), where he was sent with a small band of Sikhs to help Bhadur Shah in the war of succession. He accompanied Guru Gobind Singh to Nanded and was with him at the time of his death on 07 October 1708. Dharam Singh died at Nanded in 1708. A Gurdwara at Nanded is jointly dedicated to the memory of Bhai Dharam Singh and his companion Bhai Daya Singh.

**3. Bhai Himmat Singh** (1661-1705), one of the *Panj Payare* (Five Beloved Ones), was born at Jagannath Puri (Orissa), in 1661, in a low-caste family of watercarriers. He came to Anandpur at the young age of

17 and attached himself to Guru Gobind and his Sikhs. After coming into the fold of the Khalsa, on 29 March 1699, he became Himmat Singh. Himmat Rai, now Himmat Singh proved to be a brave, loyal and steadfast warrior, with courage, determination, and perseverance. He took part in practically all the actions fought by Guru Gobind Singh and laid down his life, fighting in the Battle of Chamkaur (07 December 1705).

**4. Bhai Mokham Singh** (1663-1705), 1663 born, son of Tirath Chand, a cloth printer of Dwarka (Gujrat), came to Anandpur around 1685. Anandpur was then the seat of Guru Gobind Singh; Mokham Chand adapted to the life and ways of the Sikhs and learnt the art of warfare there. He was one of the first five (*Panj Payare* - Five beloved Ones) to become a Khalsa on 29 March 1699 and became Mokham Singh from Mokham Chand. He took part in almost all the actions fought by Guru Gobind Singh and died fighting in the Battle of Chamkaur (07 December 1705).

**5. Bhai Sahib Singh** (1665-1705), was a barber of Bidar (Karnataka). Guru Nanak had visited Bidar early in the sixteenth century and a shrine had been established there in his memory and honour. Sahib Chand's parents (Bhai Guru Narayan and Ankamma) were aware of Baba Nanak and his preaching. Sahib Chand travelled to Anandpur at the young age of sixteen (16) and stayed put there. He learned the art of warfare and won a name for himself as a marksman. In one of the battles of Anandpur, he shot dead the Gujjar chief Jamatulla and in another action the raja of Hindur, Bhup Chand, was seriously wounded by a shot from his musket following which the entire hill army fled the battlefield. Sahib Chand was one of the first five Sikhs who, on the Baisakhi day of 29 March 1699, offered himself to Guru Gobind Singh and after undergoing the rites of the Khalsa became one of the *Panj Payare* (Five beloved Ones; the nucleus of Khalsa brotherhood) and his new name was Sahib Singh (a surname common to all members of the Khalsa fraternity) instead of Sahib Chand. Sahib Singh fell fighting in the battle of Chamkaur on 07 December 1705.

**Besides the *Panj Payare* (Five Beloved Ones), ten other eminent Sikhs who played a conspicuous role in the movement of Guru Gobind Singh are:**

**6. Jiwan Singh Rangretha (aka Bhai Jetha)** (1649 – 1705), became a Khalsa in 1699. He was born on 30 November 1649 and his parents (Sada Chand and Karmo) named him Jag Chand, from this he got his nick/pet name Jagu or Jota; in 1691 he was married to Raj Kaur, daughter of Sujan Singh of village Riar, near Amritsar and had four sons. Bhai Jaita, a Delhite, belonged to the Dalit (Ranghareta) caste and he and his brother Bhag Chand (Bhagu) were devoted disciples of Guru Har Rai. When Bhai Jaita brought the severed head of Guru Tegh Bahadur to Guru Gobind in Anandpur, the Guru said, "Ranghareta, Guru Ka Beta." (Ranghareta are the sons of the Guru). Bhai Jiwan Singh took part in almost all the battles of Guru Gobind. It was almost first light, on **06 December 1705**, when the enemy caught up with the Guru's caravan, close to the banks of River Sarsa. Bhai Jiwan Singh Rangreta (1649-1705) with a hundred men fought another (the first one was at Shahi Tibbi by Bhai Udai Singh) action to harass and delay the pursuers. He attained martyrdom in the Battle of Chamkaur on 07 December 1705. A *burj* or tower stands on the site as a monument to his memory.

**7. Bhai Mani Singh** (d. 1737) – was a scholar, martyr, and companion of Guru Gobind Singh. He was a pious and venerable head priest and custodian of the Golden Temple. It was with the assistance of Bhai Mani Singh as a scribe that Guru Gobind Singh gave final shape to the Guru Granth by incorporating the writings of his father (Guru Tegh Bahadur) in it, in 1706, at Talwandi Sabo. Bhai Mani Singh also compiled the Dasam Granth under the guidance of Guru Gobind Singh. In 1737 Zakariya Khan, the governor of Lahore granted him permission to hold the Diwali festival at Amritsar on payment of Rs five thousand as tax. This was a ruse, because on the other hand the governor sent a strong force under Diwan Lakhpat Rai to annihilate the Sikhs when they would assemble for the festival. Mani Singh came to know of this. So he forbade the Sikhs from leaving their scattered forest and desert abodes to gather at Amritsar. When the tax could not be paid Bhai Mani Singh was given the choice to either embrace Islam or face death. He chose the latter and was executed with his body mangled bone by bone. In Lahore, at the site of his martyrdom, a Gurudwara - Shahid Ganj was constructed. In recent times, another memorial gurdwara has been raised near Longowal, which is believed to be his birthplace.

**8. Bhai Nand Lal** (1633-1713), was a famous poet in the Sikh tradition and a favourite disciple of Guru Gobind Singh. His poetry, all in Persian except for *Joti Bigas*, which is in Punjabi, forms part of the approved Sikh canon and can be recited along with scriptural verse at Sikh religious *divans* (lit. a bed; a symposium of singing of poetic verses). Nand Lal used the nom de plume (pen name) "Goya", though at places he has also used 'Lal', the word being the last part of his name.

Nand Lal's father, Munshi Chhajju Mall was an official in the secretariat of Prince Dara Shukoh, Emperor Shah Jahan's eldest son and he accompanied him on an expedition to Ghazni in 1639. Munshi Chhajju Mall was assigned to an army unit stationed there at the end of the operation. He summoned his family from India to join him in Ghazni where his son, Nand Lal spent his childhood and early youth. After his father's death in 1652, Nand Lal was offered a post in Ghazni, but he declined to accept it and returned to Multan, his ancestral home. In Multan, by sheer dint of his ability and hard work Nand Lal gradually worked his way up to deputy governor of the province and eventually secured an appointment on the personal staff of Prince Muazzam, Aurangzeb's eldest son.

It cannot be exactly determined when he relinquished service. According to *Guru kian Sakhian*, Nand Lal arrived in Anandpur on Baisakhi day of 29 March 1682. There is a tradition preserved among his descendants that when the King of Persia sent a dispatch to Aurangzeb, the Emperor invited his courtiers to draft a reply. Nand Lal's draft was deemed the most suitable and was selected for dispatch to Tehran. Impressed by the Hindu's learning, Aurangzeb thought it his duty to save the soul of the 'infidel' by converting him to Islam. The most likely reason why Nand Lal left Delhi and came to the shelter of Guru Gobind Singh was to seek peace during his advancing years. Guru Gobind's fame had spread far and wide as the protector of dharma (the path of righteousness) and the son of the martyr Guru Tegh Bahadur.

Nand Lal spent his days with the Guru in mystical contemplation and composing poetry in which his spiritual experience was the pre-eminent element. He is said to have kept a good langar (free kitchen) at Anandpur which was commended by Guru Gobind as a model for others to follow. By caste Nand Lal was a Khatri, a class distinguished in Mughal times, like Kayasthas, for proficiency in Persian, which at that time was the language of official business. He appears to have been Guru Gobind's sole Persian poet.

Nand Lal was a scholar, learned in the traditional disciplines of the time, and his image in Sikh history is that of a man loved and venerated. After the Guru evacuated Anandpur in the winter of 1705, Bhai Nand Lal went to his original home at Multan where he occupied himself with preaching the Guru's word and teaching Arabic and Persian. For the latter purpose he opened a regular school which was in existence until the occupation of Punjab by the British in 1849. Nand Lal remained a Sahajdhari Sikh and never became a Khalsa. Among his writings may be mentioned *Zindagi Namah, Ganj Namah, Joti Bigas, Rahitnama, Tankhahnama, Dasturul-Insha, Arz ul-Alfaz, Diwan-i-Goya,* and the *Rubaiyat.* Nand Lal died in Multan in 1713.

**9. Bhai Batchittar Singh** (d. 1705), warrior and martyr, was the second of five sons of Bhai Mani Ram, a Parmar Rajput and a devout Sikh. The five brothers had been put at the service of Guru Gobind Singh by their father, Bhai Mani Ram. Bhai Bachittar Singh joined the order of the Khalsa on the very first day of its inception, on the Baisakhi of 29 March 1699 and shot into prominence during the first battle of Anandpur against the hill chieftains, when, on 01 September 1700, he volunteered to face a drunken elephant that had been brought by the enemy to smash the gate of Lohgarh Fort. As the elephant neared the gate, Bhai Bachittar Singh struck a powerful blow on its head with his spear that it pierced the plate and badly injured the animal. The elephant turned back, trampling the besiegers, and creating havoc in their ranks. Bachittar Singh took part in the actions at Nirmohgarh and Basoli and in the last battle of Anandpur. On the fateful night of 5/6 December 1705, when Anandpur was evacuated, he was one of those who safely crossed the Sarsa, a hill torrent near Ropar that was in spate. He commanded a flank guard watching pursuers from the direction of Ropar. Bachittar Singh was gravely injured in an encounter with the enemy. He was carried by Sahibzada Ajit Singh (elder son of the Guru) to Kotla Nihang Khan where he succumbed to his wounds two days later, on 08 December 1705.

**10. Bhai Udai Singh** (d. 1705), brother of Batchittar Singh was a warrior and Martyr. He was the third of the five sons of Bhai Mani Ram, a Parmar Rajput of Alipur in Multan district (now in Pakistan). On the day of inauguration of the Khalsa (29 March 1705), Udai Singh and his four brothers received the rites of Khalsa. He was among the trusted 25 who constituted Guru Gobind Singh's escort and took a leading part in battles fought in and around Anandpur after the creation of the Khalsa.

Udai Singh was a brave and daring man. He shot a tiger during the chase; wounded Balia Chand, who along with another hill chieftain, Alam Chand, had surprised and attacked Guru Gobind, while hunting in the valley; in the first battle of Anandpur (1700), he first strengthened the defenses and then took over the command of the reserve; it was he who introduced Sahibzada Ajit Singh (the eldest son of Guru Gobind Singh) to his first baptism in steel. Udai Singh fought valiantly in the battle that ensued and although wounded severely during the first day's battle, he participated in the night attack launched against the besieger and the following day slew Raja Kesri Chand of Jaswan in a duel. He fought with similar distinction in the battles of Nirmohgarh, Basoli and Kalmot and in the last (sixth) battle of Anandpur.

During the exodus (5/6 night of December 1705) after vacating Anandpur, Udai Singh and his fifty companions were killed, fighting desperately with a pursuing enemy (vastly superior in number), in a rearguard action. The encounter took place at a small mound called Shahi Tibbi, 6 km south of Kiratpur; though a delaying action, it is also referred to as the Battle of Shahi Tibbi. A small Gurdwara at Shahi Tibbi, now honours his memory.

**11. Bhai Mahan Singh** (d. 1705), was one of the forty martyrs of the Battle of Khidrana (29 December 1705). During the Battle of Khidrana, the forty men, who had deserted the Guru during the siege of Anandpur, came to retrieve their lost prestige; they fought like ferocious tigers and took a heavy toll of the enemy forces. Finally, the gallant forty, fighting an overwhelmingly large foe, fell dead or lay mortally wounded. After the battle, when Guru Gobind Singh went down from the hillock to scan the battlefield, he found no enemy and **Bhai Mahan Singh**, the leader of the forty, still alive. Mahan Singh died with his head in the Guru's lap. His last wish was that the Guru tear up the disclaimer and Guru Gobind willingly obliged. These forty are known as the *Chali muktas* (the emancipated ones) and as tribute to the martyrs, the Guru named the tank of Khidrana, *Muktsar* – the "Pool of Salvation." Hence the Battle of Khidrana is also known as the Battle of Muktsar.

**12. Baba Deep or Dip Singh** (1682-1757), the founder of the Shahid *misl* or principality as well as Damdami Taksal (school of Sikh learning), was born in 1682 and belonged to village Pahuvind, 40 km southwest of Amritsar. He received the vows of the Khalsa at Anandpur where he stayed for some time to study the sacred texts under Bhai Mani Singh. He rejoined Guru Gobind Singh at Talwandi Sabo in 1706 and after the latter's departure for the South, stayed on there to look after the sacred shrine, Damdama Sahib.

Later, with a small group of warriors, he joined Banda Singh Bahadur, but parted ways with him in 1714 along with a breakaway group known as Tatt Khalsa. In 1726, he had four copies of the Guru Granth made from the original one prepared by Bhai Mani Singh. In 1748, when *jathas* (fighting groups/squads) were designated as *misls* (12 in number), Baba Deep Singh headed the *Shahid* (Martyr) *misl*. This *misl* had its sphere of influence in the south of River Sutlej and its headquarters at Talwandi Sabo (Damdama Sahib). The tower in which Deep Singh lived still stands next to the Takht Sri Damdama Sahib and is known as Burj Baba Deep Singh Sahahid.

During his fourth invasion of India in the winter of 1756-57, Ahmad Shah Abdali annexed the Punjab to his Afghan dominions and appointed his son, Taimur, viceroy at Lahore, with the veteran general, Jahan Khan, as his deputy. In May 1757, Jahan Khan invested Amritsar, razed the Sikh fortress of Ram Rauni and filled up the sacred pool. As soon as the news of the desecration reached Baba Deep Singh, he set out with his *jatha* for the Holy City. On the way many Sikhs joined him, till the numbers swelled to 5,000. The two adversaries clashed at Gohlvar village, 08 km from Tarn Taran on **11 November 1757**. In the fierce action that ensued, Deep Singh suffered a mortal injury to his jugular vein, near Ramsar. His head was almost severed from his body. Yet so firm was his resolve to reach the holy precincts that he fought his way through, till he fell dead in the close vicinity of the holy temple. A legend grew that it was Baba Deep Singh's headless body holding his decapitated head on his left hand and wielding his *khanda*, (double-edged sword), with his right hand that had fought on until he had redeemed his pledge to liberate the holy shrine. So potent was the legend that over the years it began to be distorted and magnified, that it became difficult for an interested observer to separate the man from the myth.

It must be emphasised that Baba Deep Singh was an old man of 75 years, but he still led all the rest from the front. In those days, when modern amenities did not exist, extensive walking was an indispensible necessity; agriculture demanded a great degree of physical labour; people were simple and ate wholesome food; in other words, survival demanded physical robustness and the times accommodated only the strong and the sturdy. Baba Deep Singh belonged to this stock of people.

Two shrines, today, commemorate this martyr, one on the circumambulatory terrace of the *sarovar* (pond) surrounding the Golden Temple where he finally fell and the other, Shahidganj Baba Deep Singh Sahahid, near Gurdwara Ramsar, where his body was cremated.

**13. Bhai Kanhaiya** (1648-1718*),* was born in a Dhamman Khatri family of Sodhara near Wazirabad in Sialkot district (now in Pakistan). His father was a wealthy trader, but he himself being of a religious bent of mind left home when still very young and roamed about with sadhus and ascetics in search of spiritual peace. He happened to be visiting Anandpur, during the Battle of Anandpur (1705). He went around the battlefield serving water to the wounded and dying, every day, without distinction of friend or foe. Some Sikhs complained about him to Guru

Gobind Singh. On being questioned, he replied that he saw no Sikhs or Mughals, but the Guru's face in everyone. The Guru was pleased and after blessing Bhai Kanhaiya, Guru Gobind Singh, told him that he had comprehended the teachings of Sikhism profoundly and that he should keep on serving humanity to the best of his ability as long as he could.
After the Battle of Anandpur, Bhai Kanhaiya retired to his native place (Sodhara) and established a *dharamshala* at Kavha village (Attock district, now in Pakistan), which he turned into a preaching center. He founded the **Sewapanthi order**, and his special mission was selfless service to humanity at large with no discrimination whatsoever.

**14. Pandit Kirpa Singh Dutt** (d. 1705), was born Kirpa Ram Dutt and aka **Pandit Kirpa Ram**. He was the son of Bhai Aru Ram, a Saraswati Brahmin of Matan, 65 km east of Srinagar, in Kashmir. Aru Ram had met Guru Har Rai and sought his blessing at the time of the latter's visit to Kashmir in 1660. On 25 May 1675, Kirpa Ram, heading a deputation of sixteen Kashmiri Brahmins met Guru Tegh Bahadur to seek his support against the atrocities of Aurangzeb. After Guru Tegh Bahadur's arrest and martyrdom in Delhi, Kirpa Ram returned to Anandpur. According to chronicles, Pandit Kirpa Ram Dutt helped Guru Gobind Singh in his Sanskrit studies. When Guru Gobind Singh formed the Khalsa, in 1699, Pandit Kirpa Ram Dutt became Kirpa Singh. Pandit Kirpa Singh Khalsa died a martyr in the Battle of Chamkaur on 7 December 1705. His descendants live in Delhi.

**15. Mai (Mother) Bhago**, the sole survivor of the battle of Khidrana or Muktsar (29 December 1705), was a descendant of Pero Shah, the younger brother of Bhai Lengha, a Dhillon Jatt who had converted a Sikh during the time of Guru Arjan. Born at village Jhabal (Amritsar district, Punjab), she was married to Nidhan Singh Varaich of Patti. A staunch Sikh by birth and upbringing, she was pained to find that forty Sikhs from her area, who had gone to Anandpur to fight for Guru Gobind Singh, had deserted him under adverse conditions. She collected the Sikhs and goaded them to return to the Guru and redeem their sins. More than that, she led them personally. On reaching Khidrana they found the imperial army about to reach the site where the Guru and his Sikhs had entrenched themselves. The forty deserters reached on time to receive the enemy in the bushes below a mound. For them it was a matter of do or die for they had to retrieve their lost prestige. They took the enemy head on and fought tooth and nail to the last man. In the end, after taking a heavy toll of the enemy forces, the gallant forty fell dead or lay mortally wounded. Guru Gobind Singh had supported them with showers of arrows from the mound.

After the **Battle of Muktsar** (the pool of salvation), **Bhai Mahan Singh**, the leader of the forty, died in the Guru's lap. His last wish was that the Guru tear up the disclaimer and the Guru willing obliged. The lady, Mai Bhago also lay wounded, but she survived. These forty are known as the *Chali muktas* (the emancipated ones). Mai Bhago thereafter stayed on with Guru Gobind Singh as one of his bodyguard, in male attire. After the death of Guru Gobind Singh (07 October 1708), she moved further south and settled down at Jinvara, 11 km from Bidar in Karnataka, where immersed in meditation, she lived to attain a ripe old age. Her hut in Jinvara has been converted into Gurdwara Tap Asthan Mai Bhago. At Nanded, too, a hall within the compound of Takhat Sachkhand, Sri Hazur Sahib marking the site of her residence is known as Bunga Mai Bhago.

**References:**


1. The Encyclopedia of Sikhism – Harbans Singh (Editor-in Chief)
2. Sikhism: Glimpses and Glances (Volume 1) – Bhupender Singh
3. History of the Sikhs and their Religion (Volume 1) – Edited by Kirpal Singh and Kharak Singh (published by SGPC)
4. A History of the Sikhs (Volume 1) – Khushwant Singh
5. Internet (Wikipedia, the free encyclopedia)

# 12

## SAHAJDHARI SIKHS

The word Sahajdhari is composed of two words Sahaj and dhari. The word Sahaj implies serenity, equipoise, and no ego, i.e., where one resides in a state of complete peace and tranquility. The word dhari means to accede, adopt, or embrace. Thus, Sahajdhari means a person who is calm, collected, composed and unmoved by changes in circumstances or the ups and downs of life. In other words, it means a phlegmatic, sang-froid or placid individual.

As per the *Encyclopedia of Sikhism* one finds that the *Sahajdhari* word is derived from two root words *saha* (together) and *ja* (born). Hence meaning born together (with oneself) or innate. Therefore, it literally stands for an inborn nature that is not affected by outside influences that ruffle and disturb the peace of mind. This state is achieved through meditation on the True Name, spiritual discipline, and detachment in all one's actions.

Though the word *sahaj* occurs frequently in Sri Guru Granth Sahib, there is no mention of the word *Sahajdhari* in the scripture. The word came into use at a later stage. However, the word is extensively used among the Sikhs. Apparently, the word came in vogue after Guru Gobind Singh formed the Khalsa on Basakhi day, in 1699. Those who did not accept the changes (Five K's) brought about by Guru Gobind Singh began thereafter to be addressed as *Sahajdhari* (those who take time to change or those who take it easy) Sikhs as opposed to the *Singh/Kesh Dhari/Amrit Dhari/*Khalsa Sikhs. Later the British called them the Sikhs of Nanak and the Sikhs of Gobind.

The authors of *A Short History of the Sikhs* (p. 110) maintain that the term *Sahijdhari* came in to use during the period of repression or persecution of Sikhs (1716-1753); until then, the word for a clean-shaven Sikh was ***Khulasa*** as distinct from the **Khalsa**. Thus, the term

*Sahajdhari* came into use after 1716 when the Sikhs were forced to leave their homes because of repression and persecution (1716-1753). The Khalsa were of unshorn locks and *Khulasa* of shorn hair. During British times the *Sahajdhari* Sikhs were called the Sikhs of Nanak and the Khalsa Sikhs, the Sikhs of Gobind. **Hence, not all Sikhs belong to the Khalsa order**. All Khalsa are Sikhs, but all Sikhs are not Khalsa.

In his *Mahankosh*, the scholarly gentleman of letters, Bhai Kahan Singh Nabha has variously given the definition of ***Sahajdhari*** as follows: *a spiritually enlightened person*; *one who decides to adopt an easier way of life* and *a group of people among the Sikh community who do not partake of Khande-de-Pahul (baptism) and do not subscribe to the discipline of kirpan and a specially designed drawers (kachchh), but have faith only in Guru Granth Sahib and in no other scripture*.

In the footnote to the last definition, Bhai Kahan Singh ji writes:
*In the provinces of Punjab and Sind, Sahajdhari are in large numbers. Sahajdharis of Sind are known to be great faithfuls. Those among the Singhs, who look down upon the Sahajdharis are ignorant of the tenets of Sikh faith.*

Again, talking about *Sahajdharis*, Bhai Kahan Singh Nabha writes on (page 111) page one hundred eleven of the Gurmat Martand:
*All the Singhs and Sahajdharis are Nanakpanthi and are a part and parcel of the Sikh community. Let us not look down upon them and give them due respect considering them to be in the process of joining the Khalsa Sikh community slowly and gradually. This is my earnest request with folded hands.*

Respecting the tradition of S*ahijdharis,* Bhai Kahan Singh makes an earnest appeal to maintain this valuable tradition. According to Kavi Sainapat, a court poet of Guru Gobind Singh, the Guru did not coerce any Sikh to join the Khalsa Panth, it was their will and wish. It appears that those who decided not to partake of Amrit at that time came to be known as S*ahijdharis* in Sikh tradition.

There is no doubt that the contribution of Sahajdhari Sikhs in Sikh history has been great. Bhai Nand lal and Bhai Kanhaiya were the two most respected Sahajdhari Sikhs of Guru's time. Among some of the other prominent *Sahajdharis* in Sikh history are **Dewan Todar Mal**, who vertically laid gold coins on a piece of land, as a price for the land required for the last rites of the martyred sahibzadas and the revered mother of the Guru. The land thus bought is recorded to be the costliest in the history of the whole world. As an expression of gratitude for such veneration and service, a hall has been constructed at Fatehgarh Sahib and named 'Dewan Todar Mal Hall' to commemorate the sacred memory of such a devotee.

Then, there was **Bhai Moti Lal Mehra**, who sacrificed his whole family just to serve milk to Mata Gujri and her two grandsons, when they were kept hungry for days in severe cold. Another *Sahajdhari* **Bhai Des Raj** was entrusted with the duty of constructing Sri Darbar Sahib, Amritsar, after it was demolished by Ahmad Shah Abdali in 1762. **Bhai Vasti Ram**, a learned man, well versed in Sikh scripture enjoyed considerable respect in the court of Maharaja Ranjit Singh. Such is the well-deserved respect given to *Sahajdharis* in Sikh tradition.

**Bhai Nand Lal** (1633-1713), was a great Persian scholar and poet and favourite disciple of Guru Gobind Singh, who also maintained a langar in his house at Anandpur, which was open to all visitors 24 hours a day. Once, while on inspection of the quality of langar being run by Sikhs in their homes, Guru Gobind found the langar being served in the house of Bhai Nand Lal was of the best quality. In 1696, when Aurangzeb ordered his son Muazzam to take out a punitive expedition for the restoration of law and order and recovery of unpaid tribute, Muazzam (later Bahadur Shah) deputed Mirza Beg to teach a lesson to the hill chiefs. The Guru was not touched; Mirza Beg had secret instructions not to bother the Guru. As per Sikh chronicles this was brought about by the good offices of Bhai Nand Lal "Goya," the *Sahajdhari* Sikh poet of Persian, who had influence over the prince.

**Kaura Mall**, Diwan, Maharaja Bahadur (d.1752), a (Arora - Chuggh), *Sahajdhari* Sikh and trusted officer under Mughals in eighteenth century Punjab, was the son of Vallu Ram, originally from a village near Shorkot in Jhang district (now in Pakistan). When Lakhpat Rai, the diwan of Lahore embarked on the dastardly path of extermination of the Sikhs, it was Kaura Mall who pleaded for them. When Mu'in ul-Malik (Mir Manu) became governor in 1748, he appointed Diwan Kaura Mal, as his minister; Kaura Mal procured custody of Lakhpat Rai and handed him over to the Sikhs. Lakhpat Rai was thrown into a dungeon where he died a miserable death after six months of indignities and torture.

Diwan Kaura Mall was addicted to smoking the hubble-bubble (*hukkah*) and the Nihangs imposed a daily fine of Rs 5/- on him. However, he was a staunch Sikh, who made no secret of his attachment to the faith of Nanak. Kaura Mall, in fulfillment of his promise to the Sikhs, constructed Gurdwara Bal Lila and a *sarowar* (tank) at Nanaka Sahib and got the pool at Darbar Sahib, Amritsar desilted; the pool had been filled up by Lakhpat Rai. On the advice of Kaura Mall, Mir Manu offered to **give the Sikhs a *jagir*** if they agreed to remain peaceful. Kaura Mal fell fighting the Afghans, on 06 March 1752. Diwan Kaura Mall is an ancestor of the renowned and famous Sikh poet, scholar, and exegete Bhai Vir Singh (1872-1957), who is accredited to be the creator of modern Punjabi literature and a prominent figure in Singh Sabha Movement.

*Sahajdharis* have all along been participating in Sikh affairs by associating with Sikh Institutions and Organisations. There used to be *Sahajdhari* committees of different regions. A *Sahajdharis'* meeting formed a part of proceedings of Sikh Educational Conferences held by Chief Khalsa Dewan. **Dr Harbans Lal**, a noted scholar, remained president of All India Sikh Students Fedration. He continues to contribute research articles on Sikh Studies to various Sikh journals. It is mentioned in *Encyclopedia of Sikhism* that Singh Sabha used to have seats reserved on the executive committees for Sahajdharis. Three presidents of *Sarab Hind Sahajdhari Confrence* namely, Mahant Karam Chand, Bhai Sant Ram and Bhai Ram Lal Rahai eventually took the vows of Khalsa Baptism and were respectively given the names Gurdarshan Singh, Sant Ram Singh and Ramlal Singh Rahai.

Earlier, *Sahajdhari* and other Sikhs were allowed to vote in the S.G.P.C. elections. But today, not only they but many sagacious Sikhs keep aloof. There is no mention of the word *Sahajdhari* in the *Sikh Rehat Maryada* (Sikh code of conduct) published by SGPC and since there is no mention of *Sahajdhari* supporting unshorn hair and beard as shown in the photographs in the *Mahankosh*, this amendment in the Sikh Gurdwara Act about the definition of a *Sahajdhari,* prompted the Sikh leaders to disallow them in 2001 from voting, for fear of non Sikhs becoming voters in the Gurdwara elections.

In October 2003, the central government passed a notification debarring *Sahajdhari* Sikhs from voting in the Gurdwara elections. *Sahajdharis* Sikh Federation filed a petition in the Punjab and Haryana High Court which was dismissed on technical grounds. The matter was then referred to Supreme Court and now with the bill debarring the *Sahajdharis* from voting having been passed in both houses of Parliament, the way has been paved for the implementation of the notification.

As far as the use of the word *Sahajdhari* is concerned, it does not occur anywhere either in Guru Granth Sahib or in *Sikh Rehat Maryada* published by SGPC. It appears the word came to be used by Sikhs for those who for certain reasons were not yet prepared for the Khanda (double edged sword) Baptism and had postponed the decision to do so at a later date, and for this very reason, came to be known as *Sahajdharis* the people who were preparing themselves for the Baptism slowly and gradually.

Keeping of hair is the most important tenet of the Sikh faith for which the Sikhs did not shy away even from laying down their lives. The forces inimical to Sikhs understood this too well. That is the reason that during their days of persecution, the Sikhs were given only one choice, either to cut their hair or face death. No such choice was given in the case of other articles of faith. The Sikhs always chose death rather than cut their hair.

The Sikh Gurudwara Act 1925 came into force on 01 November 1925. When the ibid bill was being passed in the Punjab Legislative Council, two august gentlemen (Sir Fazal-i-Hussain and Lord Malcolm Hailley, the then governor and chairman of Assembly) warned the Sikhs of the consequences of the bill. Their predictions are proving true today. Instead of an election system an **Electoral College** would have suited and proved much better.

Except Sikhism, no other religion in the world has an electoral system. This system has failed miserably, it has only helped in concentrating political and spiritual powers in the hands of a few and in serving their vested interests and ulterior motives. And, now with the law barring Sahajdhari Sikhs (including other Sikhs too) from voting has divided the community and also the rich and immensely meaningful range of beliefs of the Sikh religion by making followers choose between the legacy of Guru Nanak and Guru Gobind. The law came into force w.e.f 08 October 2003 and was decided solely according to the Sikh *Rehat Maryada* (code of conduct and conventions). Self-appointed 'messengers of God' have assumed the role of middlemen and taken over the religion; spirituality has been thrown into the background and outward appearance has taken precedence over religious teachings and deeper understanding. A modern faith has been reduced to a bodily artifact.

Because of the Five K's, even Sahajdharis, Punjabi monas (clean shaven) and Sindhis, who revere the Gurus and recite Gurbani, have come to be regarded as non-Sikhs. Actually they are Sikhs (Shishyas) alright; only, they are not Khalsa with long unshorn hair, etc. Though Guru Nanak is believed to be the Guru of the Sikhs, there are millions of others who love and believe in him, and worship him. Among Hindus, Muslims and other religions there are **'Nanak Panthies'** by hundreds and thousands. Not counting the Sahajdharis, Nanak Panthies and other dispensations as Sikhs will be an irreparable loss that the Sikh community cannot afford. This large number will enrich and strengthen the Sikh community. They would also add to the Sikh demographic figures - always needed in a democratic set-up of governance. These people may be better and true

Sikhs than the claimant Sikhs (Khalsa) themselves. So it would be a gross mistake to ignore the writing on the wall and the lessons of history. What the Sikhs forget is that it the voice of the people, the majority and the numbers that count in a democratic country.

It may be a very sensitive and religious issue, but it requires immediate attention of the Moguls in the corridors of SGPC. They must address the problem at the earliest and a solution must be found. If these people are not allowed to vote, then my suggestion is that seats should be reserved for the Sahajdharis, the Nanak Panthis, the Sindhis, the Udasis, and the Nirmalas and even for the Lamas, who once came in hordes to the Golden Temple and other Gurdwaras and also the rest of the dispensations that have not been mentioned.

**References:**

1. The Encyclopedia of Sikhism – Harbans Singh (Editor-in Chief)
2. History of the Sikhs and their Religion (Volume 1) – Edited by Kirpal Singh and Kharak Singh (published by SGPC).
3. A History of the Sikhs (Volume 1) – Khushwant Singh
4. A Short History of The Sikhs (Volume 1) – Teja Singh and Ganda Singh
5. Sikhism: Glimpses and Glances (Volume 1) – Bhupender Singh
6. Editorial on Sahajdhari Sikhs in July – September 2016 issue of Abstracts of Sikh Studies
7. Internet (Wikipedia, the free encyclopedia)

**You don't know where you are going; until you know where you are coming from.**

**— Native American saying**

# 13

## GURU GOBIND SINGH'S HORSE - DILBAG

Horses have always formed part of mankind's glorious history; various warriors have won many wars with their favourite horses. Some names of horses that became famous in history are: Lord Buddha's **Kanthaka**, Maharana Pratap's **Chetak**, Maharaja Ranjit Singh's **Laila** (a Persian mare known as **Asp-i-Laila** that cost him **Rupees 60 lakhs and 12,000 soldiers)**, Rani Laxmibai's **Badal**, Alexander's **Bucephalus**, Napoleon Bonaparte's **Marengo** and **Viziror "LeVizir"**, Wellington's Copenhagen and many more.

There is mention of horses at many places in the Guru Granth Sahib. To improve the economic condition of Sikhs, Guru Arjan Dev encouraged them to trade (especially in horses). The importance of horses and horse-riding in Sikhism is perhaps best summed up by the Sikh Code of Conduct (*Rehat Maryada*) which is based on 52 edicts (*hukam namas*) issued by Guru Gobind Singh at Nanded in 1708. These edicts give the ideal way of life for the Khalsa. **Hukam 30 says: 'Learn and train in the skills of weaponry and horse riding'.**

In view of the prevailing, turbulent times, like his grandfather, Guru Hargobind, Guru Gobind instructed the Sikhs to make offerings of arms and horses. And, in anticipation of the tumultuous and stormy period ahead, Guru Gobind Singh acquired equestrian skills (horsemanship) from an early age under the guidance of his maternal uncle, Bhai Kirpal Chand. As the Guru grew older, he became an accomplished horseman and would spend time travelling the countryside on horseback.

Guru Gobind Singh was famous for his blue-coloured horse, **Dilbag** (Neela Ghora) and Dilbag, the blue horse had become a legend on account of its agility, boldness, steadfastness, and intelligence. Many folk songs and *vars* (ballad, composition, poem, or verse) sing the exploits of *"Neelay ghoray they swaar"* or *"the rider of the blue horse"*.

The *beau ideal* of the Punjabis, Guru Gobind Singh was a handsome man, whose feats as a cavalier; swordsman and archer were enough to endear him to a people who gauged a man by his physical prowess. He became a legendary figure in his lifetime and the Punjabis pictured him leading them to battle on a roan stallion. One of their favourite titles for him was, the rider of the blue horse (*nile ghore da asvar*). It is not clear from where the blue horse, **Dilbag** affectionately known as *Neela* (meaning "blue"), was acquired. It may have been a gift from a royal dignitary or from a devotee.

The colour of blue roan horses (the breed to which **Dilbag** belonged) is officially known as Blue Roan. A Blue Roan is a dark-coloured horse with the roan gene. The roan gene gives the horse interspersed white hair on his body and this gives a general blue hue or sheen to the horse. The legs and occasionally the head of the horse are not affected and will remain darker than the body. The mane and tail are also usually not affected, but some horses may have some white hair mixed in. Roan is a stable colouration throughout life. Blue Corn is a variation of Blue Roan, in which speckles and spots of the base colour (black) appear, making a mottled appearance.

To this day, the lineage of the stallions of horse **Dilbag** (*Neela Ghora*) continues at Hazoor Sahib, Nanded. The horses are kept in stables and bred down from the original stallion belonging to the Guru, although, over time the blue colour has been diluted down to a grey white. No one is allowed to ride the horses as a mark of respect, and they are brought out on the festival of *Holla Mahalla* (festival of Holi celebrated by Sikhs with mock battles and martial arts) or *Gurpurbs* (birth/death anniversaries of Gurus) when they are beautifully decorated with tassels and riding gear. **Anmol** is the present horse bred down a number of generations from **Dilbag** (Neela Ghora), the 'father' and original horse of the tenth Guru. During the *Baisakhi* (spring harvest and birth of Khalsa, celebrated on 13 April) celebrations, Anmol is adorned with a *Kalgi* (aigrette, crest, hackle, panache, plume, or tuft), dressed up stylishly and takes part in the celebrations. On occasions, especially on the festival of *Holla Mahalla*, it is said that the horse will get extremely sweaty and agitated, as if it is being ridden.

**Five short stories of the Guru's Blue Horse, Dilbag:**

**1. Gurdwara Putthi Sahib, Punjab**

This Gurdwara commemorates the incident when Guru Gobind Singh arrived at this place after a long journey, on his way back to Anandpur Sahib. They say Guru Gobind saw an artisan, working at a kiln (*putthi*) for baking bricks. Upon enquiring from him if there was a place to rest, the man gestured at his furnace and said mockingly, "If you call yourself Guru why don't you rest here in the furnace?" Serenely, the Guru ushered Neela (**Dilbag**) forward and the horse trampled on the mud surrounding the kiln and put one of his hooves on the side of the kiln. Whereas a brick kiln would normally take a week or so to cool down, the furnace became instantly cool. Guru Gobind alighted and rested for the night in the furnace. The gurdwara that now stands at the place has been built around the now solidified mud which still has the impressions of Neela's/Dilbag's hooves.

**2. Kotla Nihang Khan and the 'Rider of the Blue Horse'**

The village Kotla Nihang Khan (named after its once local chief, Nihang Khan, a God-fearing Afghan), about two and a half kilometers south of Ropar (30"58'N, 76°31'E), owes its prominence to Gurdwara Bhatta Sahib. Guru Gobind Singh first visited Kotla Nihang Khan while on his way back from Paonta to Anandpur.

The site of the present Gurdwara Bhattha Sahib used to be a *Bhattha* (a brick kiln) which was used to slake lime for mortar and whitewashing of walls. The kiln, in use at the time belonged to the local chief. It is said that the kiln was still smouldering hot when the Guru arrived there on *Magghar* (October/November) *Amavas* (dark night), or 12 November 1688 and, inadvertently or otherwise, rode right onto the kiln's covering.

There is a fascinating story about this incident. It is said that as soon as the hooves of the Guru's horse touched the kiln, it cooled down. Seeing this, Nihang Khan fell at the Guru's feet and became forever his devoted follower. He escorted him to his *haveli* (mansion) and put him up for the night with due reverence and attention.

### 3. Gurdwara Paur (Hoof) Sahib

Twelve (12) km north of Anandpur Sahib, in Bilaspur district of Himachal Pradesh is a small town called Guru Ka Lahore. It is here that the marriage of Guru Gobind Singh to Mata Jito took place in 1677. The nuptials were scheduled to take place in Lahore but the fateful events leading to the martyrdom of the ninth Guru intervened and a temporary encampment called **Guru Ka Lahore** was setup near village Basantgarh. A small Gurdwara, Anand Karaj Stan Patshahi Dasvi (location of wedding of the tenth master) marks the site where the matrimony took place. Two hundred (200) meters south of this Gurdwara, next to a spring, stands Gurdwara Paur Sahib. According to popular legend, the spring was the consequence of stamping of the hoof (*paur*, in Punjabi) of Guru Gobind Singh's horse.

### 4. Neela, the blue horse ferries the Guru across the stormy River Sarsa

The Guru passed through Kotla Nihang Khan, for a second time while returning after viewing the solar eclipse on 17 February 1703. His third visit to this place was on 6 December 1705. This time, Guru Gobind Singh, after being forced to abandon Anandpur headed straight towards Kotla Nihang Khan. The River Sarsa was in spate but his faithful horse **Dilbag** ferried him safely across the furious waters. The Guru had detached 100 of his warriors under Bhai Bachchittar Singh to cover his flank. He safely reached Kotla and, while relaxing in Nihang Khan's house, he waited for Bachchittar Singh to fetch up.

### 5. Dilbag and the tobacco field

It is said that once on reaching a tobacco field, Guru Gobind Singh's horse, **Dilbag**, bolted and refused to set foot in the tobacco cultivation. The Guru changed route and took a longer diversion. On being asked about this strange action, he replied that when **Dilbag** found tobacco repulsive and had refused to walk through the polluted and unclean place then why should he allow his Sikhs to do so? Earlier, Guru Gobind had realised the ill-effects of tobacco and when his horse also refused to enter the tobacco field, his resolve to ban tobacco for the Sikhs was further strengthened. He said, "Alcohol destroys a generation, but tobacco destroys several generations." The Sikh religion asks its followers to shun tobacco. Smoking and drug taking is banned in Sikhism and using tobacco in any form is listed in the Sikh Code of Conduct (*Rehat Maryada*) as one of the four transgressions (*Kurahits*). One cannot help but wonder and admire the wisdom and farsightedness of the Great Guru.

Right up to the early part of the last century (twentieth century), horses formed an important part of warfare and transportation of men and material. Horse riding was a vital part of the life of a human being. The Sikhs fought all battles with their steeds, but sadly, truly little or no records have been kept by them. Perhaps, it was the turbulent times that hampered them from doing so.

**Note** – Not much material on this topic is available. Besides sketchy material on the internet and a few stray lines in some books, most of the books are silent on the subject. Corrections and criticism are welcome.

**References:**


1. The Encyclopedia of Sikhism – Harbans Singh (Editor-in Chief)
2. Internet (Wikipedia, the free encyclopedia)

# 14

## SIKHS AND TOBACCO

In 6,000 BC, native Americans first started cultivating the **tobacco** plant and by circa 1 BC, indigenous American tribes started **smoking tobacco** in religious ceremonies and for medicinal purposes. Christopher Columbus first encountered dried **tobacco** leaves in 1492. They were given to him as a gift by the American Indians. Following the arrival of Europeans, tobacco became one of the primary products fueling colonization, and also became a driving factor in the incorporation of African slave labour. The Spanish introduced tobacco to Europeans in about 1528. Jean Nicot (from whose name the word nicotine derives), the French ambassador in Lisbon sent samples of tobacco to Paris in 1560. Tobacco was introduced in India by the Portuguese during the 17th century.

It may appear strange to people of other religions as to why Sikhism has such an anti-smoking stance. Of all the nations that Europeans came across, the Sikhs were the only ones who had a religious injunction against tobacco. Early European writers who came in contact with Sikhs in the 1780's were perplexed as to why tobacco was forbidden for the Sikhs as it was being widely used by both the British and the Indians at the time.

During the time of Guru Gobind Singh the use of tobacco by Mughul nobles had become common. Guru Gobind forbade his Sikhs the use of tobacco; he said that **alcohol destroys a generation but tobacco destroys several generations**. All Sikh writers, who were contemporaries of Guru Gobind Singh record smoking as being forbidden for Sikhs.

**The Sikh religion asks its followers to shun tobacco like the plague.** Smoking and drug taking is banned in Sikhism and using tobacco is listed in the Sikh *Rehat Maryada* (Code of Conduct, drafted by an expert committee of eminent Sikh scholars) as one of the four transgressions (*Kurahits*). The Sikh Code of Conduct sums up the ideal way of life of the Khalsa and is based on 52 edicts (*hukamnamas*) issued by Guru Gobind Singh at Nanded in 1708. These edicts were written by order of Guru Gobind Singh and copied down by Baba Ram Singh Koer, the great grandson of Baba Buddha. Guru Gobind Singh affixed his personal seal to the document, a copy of which can be seen at the historic Gurdwara, Paonta Sahib, built on the River Yamuna banks in the town of Paonta Sahib, Sirmaur District, Himachal Pradesh about 44 kilometers from Dehradun.

Until the 1950's smoking was encouraged by governments as a means to acquire tax. Only in 1950 when Morton Levin published his study which connected lung cancer to smoking did any government take notice. According to the World Health Organization report of 1995, worldwide lung cancer is the biggest single cause of cancer deaths in men. Smoking causes approximately 3 million deaths worldwide and if current trends persist it will kill 10 million a year from 2020. Smoking causes about 20.5% of all deaths in developed countries. These are frightening statistics, but the biggest tragedy is that smoking is the single largest preventable factor in premature death, disability, and disease. These effects of smoking are not limited to the smokers themselves but to those around them. Family, friends, and even complete strangers in the smoker's vicinity suffer. Smoking by women, while pregnant has been linked to sudden infant death syndrome (cot death), bronchitis, pneumonia, and higher risk of miscarriage.

Apart from the effects on health, smoking also takes a large chunk of family budgets sometimes as much as 20% if both parents smoke. Smoking is increasing in developing countries amongst people who can ill afford the habit. There are roughly 1.1 billion smokers worldwide, i.e., about 17% of the total population and about 6000 billion cigarettes are smoked every year. According to some estimates about 300 million is spent on the habit worldwide with about 100 billion being spent in developing countries. This sheer wastage is borne by families who live in slum quarters, unable to better themselves due to the drain on their resources caused by smoking.

It is said that once on reaching a tobacco field, Guru Gobind Singh's horse, **Dilbag**, bolted and the Guru changed route and took a longer diversion. On being asked about this strange action, he replied that when even **Dilbag** found tobacco repulsive and had refused to walk through the polluted and unclean place then why should he allow his Sikhs to do so. The Guru had already realised the ill-effects of tobacco and when his horse refused to enter the tobacco field, his resolve to ban tobacco for the Sikhs was further strengthened.

The Sikh faith asks its followers to shun tobacco and they were forbidden to associate with people who smoke. They were also not to have any social or matrimonial relations with smokers. Sikhs abhor tobacco and their religion strictly prohibits its use in all forms (it is absolutely a taboo). A Sikh should not touch tobacco. It is listed in the Sikh Code of Conduct (*Rehat Maryada*) as one of the four transgressions (*Kurahits*).

Besides smoking, drugs, wine and other intoxicants are also forbidden in the Sikh faith. M.A. Macauliffe, the gentleman who wrote the book, *The Sikh Religion* in six volumes, and was perhaps the first European to convert to Sikhism said, "It is known to every Sikh that **tobacco** is forbidden by his religion, but it is not generally known that wine is equally forbidden. After I had quoted the Sikh tenets on this subject in public lectures at Simla, it was taken up by the enlightened Singh Sabha of Patiala; and a resolution in favour of total abstinence was signed by several of the best educated and most influential Sardars of the State." - M.A. Macauliffe (preface to his book 'The Sikh Religion').

Given below are some quotes from Sikh scriptures:

*Pĝn supĝrī khĝtīĝ mukh bīrīĝ lĝīĝ.*

**'Those who eat betel nuts and betel leaf and put cigarette in mouth'**

*Har har kadė na chėtio jam pakar chalĝīĝ. ||13||*

**'and do not contemplate the Lord, Har, Har - the Messenger of Death will seize them and take them away. ||13||'**

***'Sri Guru Granth Sahib Ji:***

***"One person brings a full bottle, and another fills his cup. Drinking sharab, (alcohol), his intelligence departs, and madness enters his mind; he cannot***

***distinguish between his own and others, and he is struck down by Waheguru, his Lord and Master. Drinking it, he forgets Waheguru, his Lord and Master, and he is punished in the Court of the Lord." (Ang 554, SGGS)***

**"This body is the Temple of the Lord, in which the jewel of spiritual wisdom is revealed. The self-willed *manmukhs* do not know anything at all; they do not believe that the Lord's Temple is within. ||2||" (SGGS 1346)**

*"The Khalsa is my own form;*
*I manifest myself through the Khalsa.*
*So long as Khalsa remains distinct;*
*I bestow all glory on them."*
***(Guru Gobind Singh)***

Besides cancer, smoking has many other adverse side effects. Well over three hundred years ago, Guru Gobind Singh foresaw the miseries that would emanate from tobacco and wisely instructed the Sikhs to keep away from it. One cannot help but wonder and admire the foresight of the tenth master, Guru Gobind Singh. He foresaw the curse and agony of the tobacco plant and, the misfortunes that would stem from it. He prudently banned tobacco for his Sikhs. Such foresight is indeed befitting a great prophet.

**Note** – Not much material on this topic is available. Besides sketchy material on the internet and a few stray lines in some books, most of the books are silent on this subject. Corrections and criticism are welcome.

## References:

1. The Encyclopedia of Sikhism – Harbans Singh (Editor-in Chief)
2. The Sikh Religion (Six Volumes) – M. A. Macauliffe
3. Internet (Wikipedia, the free encyclopedia)

# 15

## SIKHS AND THE HOLY COWS

### The Background

Hindus revere the cow. The vast majority of the population of India is Hindus; if Jains, Buddhists and Sikhs are reckoned as Hindus, and there are good enough reasons for so doing, then almost 87% of India is Hindu. The Constitution of India was drafted by highly erudite Hindus many of whom had been educated at American and British universities and eaten their fill of beefsteaks and veal escallops when they were abroad. But when it came to putting it down on paper, they felt compelled to insert a directive clause in the Constitution providing for the protection of cows. This clause (couched in discreet language) is ingeniously worded so that outsiders might not snigger and call them backward:

"The State shall endeavour to organise agriculture and animal husbandry on modern and scientific lines and shall, in particular, take steps for preserving and improving the breeds, and prohibiting the slaughter of cows and calves and other milch and draught cattle."

**Cow Menace and Economic aspects of cow protection:** 235 million cows; cows dying of hunger; people dying of hunger. Cows roaming the streets and eating from garbage bins and licking urinals are a common sight in almost every part of India. Sacred cows create havoc on the streets. While stray cattle are a traffic nuisance in cities, they also raid crops in villages. Many bovine animals are abandoned forever because they are no longer of any value and urban residents drive out their cattle to wander around unrestricted and unprotected during the day. Lot of cows, die on roads due to accidents or by eating plastics and rubbish. In a *sabzi mandi* (vegetable market) cows raid and feed on unattended stalls and shops and if they run amuck, they cause havoc by attacking public and overturning handcarts. Then, there is the communicable disease called **Leptospirosis** that results in abortion and pathological changes in animal and human behavior. The disease spreads through indirect contact with contaminated urine material of bovines.

**The Hindu Viewpoint**

The Hindus consider and treat the cows as holy and sacred animals and respect and worship them. They proclaim their bovine births: *Gau hamari mata hai* (The cow is our mother). Their belief is that its (cow's) milk is essential for anyone who wants to lead a spiritual life. Cow's milk, curds, butter, and buttermilk keep a man's body healthy without exciting sex. A black cow's milk is considered better than that of a white one. Limited amount of milk used to be taken from the cow and selling milk of a household cow was considered a sin. If cows are better feed, they will yield more milk.

Cows not only give us milk, even their waste is found to be of great medicinal use. Cow dung is used to fertilize land and cow urine is full of medicinal properties. It is used in many *ayurvedic* (the traditional Hindu system of medicine) medicines. **Economics are in favour of cow protection.** Eating the flesh of an animal whose milk you drink is like eating one's mother. Consuming beef is a crime. If the government can spend ten crore (100 million) rupees on an abattoir, it can spend ten lakh (01 million) rupees on *gau shalas* (cattle pens). Secularism does not mean that the religious feelings of Hindus (who form over eighty-five percent of the population of the country), should be deliberately hurt.

Their opinion is that however westernized an Indian may be, whenever he eats beef, he will have a sense of some guilt and not one Indian will bandy words with a *sadhu* (a holy man, monk, sage, or ascetic) for fear of arousing his wrath. It is like our attitude to *suttee* (con-cremation of widows). We condemn it, but we cannot help admiring a woman who becomes a *suttee*. These things have been with us for over 4,000 years. They are inherent in us. We cannot fight them with reason. They are stronger than reason.

**A Complex problem**: *'India needs to look beyond gaushalas (cow shelters) to address its stray cattle problem.'*

Even though there have been multiple government interventions, the problem persists. But the growing number of stray cows is proving to be a bane for both citizens and their bovine gods. Nearly 7 million stray cows roam freely on India's roads and the number is expected to go up substantially.

The answer has to do with religion. Religion and cows are the vote bank of political parties. Many states already prohibit cow slaughter…… with religious zealots ready to take on anyone harming the divine creature... Violent "cow vigilantes" (*gau rashaks* or cow protectors) roam the roads, killing people, often working with police to allegedly extort money from cattle traders. The abandonment of cattle is unfortunate as they are quite an important resource, contributing to nutritional security and strengthening local livelihood.

There are several reasons for the high share of stray cattle in the country: from neglect of the indigenous populations to excessive focus on crossbreeding in the past few decades. Increased mechanisation and the national ban on cow slaughter have further added to the problem.

In common parlance, stray cattle include cows, bulls or calves that are abandoned because they are unproductive. They also include low-yield cows, mostly owned by city-dwellers that are set free to roam about in the open during the daytime. Stray cattle are a nuisance in cities and villages.

Given the complexity of the problem, simply directing stray cattle towards *gaushalas* (cow shelters) is not going to be sufficient. This is clear as the Centre has been constantly increasing the number of and support to *gaushalas* under the Rashtriya Gokul Mission with little success. Many of the owners of cow shelters are corrupt.

Seven of the 10 states with the greatest number of stray cattle have recorded a rise in their number between 2012 and 2019, suggested the Livestock Census. So evidently, the Centre needs to widen its strategy to reduce stray cattle. For this, it first needs to improve its understanding of cattle, especially of the neglected varieties that have been sidelined by their popular counterparts.

## The Sikh Faith and Cows

Except for a few stray lines by Guru Gobind Singh there is nothing to substantiate cow-worship in the Sikh scriptures. However, the **Sikhs strictly abstain from eating beef and hurting cows** (due to their genesis and intimate links with the religion of their ancestors). During Sikh rule the slaughter of kine was strictly forbidden. The foreigners in the service of Maharaja Ranjit Singh signed contracts not to shave their beards and not to smoke or eat beef. The Namdharis (sub-sect of Sikhs) are ardent protectors of cows and made it the chief point of their agitation against the British. **By tradition, no meat is served in Langars**. Although Sikhs are not vegetarians by conviction, the majority eats meat only on rare occasions and a devout Sikh refrains from smoking or taking intoxicants and is a strict vegetarian.

## Namdharis Sikhs – Protectors of Cows

Despite his criticism of many Hindu practices, Ram Singh of Bhaini, the most important and popular guru of the Namdharis, originally known as *Jagyasis* and *Abhiasis* (seekers and mediators) and later called the Kookas (from their loud shrieks or *kooks* when they worked themselves into frenzy) became an ardent protector of the cow. Ram Singh was a peace-loving saint. Much against his wishes, some Kooka fanatics murdered a few Muslim butchers and their families in Amritsar and then at Raikot (Ludhiana district). Eight Kookas were hanged, and others sentenced to long terms of imprisonment.

Kooka passions were inflamed with all the happenings around them. In January 1872 one gang ignoring their guru's advice attacked Malaund and Malerkotla (a Muslim state where cow slaughter was permitted) for arms. Their attempt failed and all 68 of them were apprehended. Mr L Cowan, the deputy commissioner of Ludhiana, who, perhaps, wished to be known as the defender of the British Empire in India, interpreted this venture as the beginning of another rebellion in the country. And, without any trial or formality, ordered forty-nine (49) of the Kookas to be blown up by tying them to the mouths of cannons, on 17 January

1872. Similarly, the commissioner of Ambala, Mr T D Forsythe, blasted off another 16 Kookas the next day.

Whatever sympathy the mainstream Sikh may have had for this revivalist movement of the Namdharis turned to anger and indifference for this misguided action of theirs and they became unsympathetic. Baba Ram Singh with 12 of his lieutenants was exiled to Rangoon where he died on 29 November 1884. Of the two English officers L Cowan was dismissed from service and the commissioner, T D Forsythe was transferred outside Punjab for this calculated cold-blooded murder.

## Two Newspaper (The Tribune) Extracts

### 1. The Nihangs and Cows

The Nihang chief, Baba Kahn Singh, addressing newsmen said that while Punjab had the unique distinction of being without any slaughterhouse, UP and other parts of the country had numerous butcheries. He regretted that certain persons who "paraded their love for the cow" had done little to close slaughterhouses in UP and elsewhere. Even more surprising was the fact that certain persons had been trading with impunity in beef, hides and skins, and possessed cold stores to keep beef. The Baba said that his sect had been looking after cows "as ordained by Guru Gobind Singh." It had a cow farm in Baba Bakala (Amritsar district) where 1,000 cows were fed.

(From the *Tribune Bureau*, Chandigarh, 03 May 1982)

### 2. How the Qadian Slaughterhouse was Destroyed and closed

It was in the late twenties/thirties of the last century, that the only slaughterhouse for cows in Punjab was set up at Qadian and was located a mile away from the main town. The Sikhs from the neighbouring villages fought a prolonged legal battle for its closure. Qadian was the headquarters of the Ahmediya sect and thus had an aura of sanctity. Under the then existing laws, and also because of the prevailing socio-religious circumstances, the Sikhs lost the legal battle. But they were not disheartened.

The Sikhs decided thereafter to act against the British government. Several thousand members of the community assembled on a dark night and marched to the slaughterhouse. They set free all the cows tethered inside and demolished the building. By daybreak, the area where the slaughterhouse once stood had been neatly ploughed and had become a part of the adjoining fields.

But that was a different time. The Sikhs never claimed that they had done a favour to their Hindu brothers. The Sikhs had always been in the forefront of the fight against cow slaughter and protecting the cows.

It is only when there is not a single cow roaming the streets of India that the problem of stray cattle will be deemed to have been solved. People releasing their animals on public roads, should be detained, fined and if need be, jailed. The government needs to take serious, concerted, stringent and pragmatic action because relying solely on cattle shelters is certainly not the answer.

**References:**


1. The Encyclopedia of Sikhism – Harbans Singh (Editor-in Chief)
2. Sikhism: Glimpses and Glances (Volume 1) – Bhupender Singh
3. Fragments of Half a Century - Karnail Singh
4. A History of the Sikhs (Volume 1) – Khushwant Singh

# BIBLIOGRAPHY


1. The Encyclopedia of Sikhism – Harbans Singh (Editor-in Chief)
2. History of the Sikhs and their Religion (Volume 1) – Edited by Kirpal Singh and Kharak Singh (published by SGPC)
3. The Sikh Religion (Six Volumes) – M. A. Macauliffe
4. A History of the Sikhs (Volume 1) – Khushwant Singh
5. A Short History of The Sikhs (Volume 1) – Teja Singh and Ganda Singh
6. Sikhism (Its Philosophy and History) - Edited by Daljeet Singh and Kharak Singh (published by Institute of Sikh Studies).
7. A Brief Account of the Sikh People - Ganda Singh
8. Sikhism: Glimpses and Glances (Volume 1) – Bhupender Singh
9. Homage to Guru Gobind Singh – Khushwant Singh and Suneet Vir Singh
10. Guru Gobind Singh – Gopal Singh
11. Evolution of the Khalsa (Two Volumes) – Indubhusan Banerjee
12. Abstracts of Sikh Studies - July-September 2016 issue
13. Abstracts of Sikh Studies - January-March 2017 issue (Guru Gobind Singh number)
14. Fragments of Half a Century - Karnail Singh
15. The Sikhs and their Scriptures – C H Loehlin
16. History of India (1000-1707 A.D.) – A L Srivastava
17. History of India – D N Kundra and S D Kundra
18. History of The Punjab - Class XII (Punjab) – Professor Manjeet Singh Sodhi
19. Social Studies Part II (History and Civics) – Class X – Punjab School Education Board
20. Glimpses of the Sikh Gurus (For Children) – Mukhtar S Goraya
21. Internet (Wikipedia, the free encyclopedia)

www.ingramcontent.com/pod-product-compliance
Lightning Source LLC
LaVergne TN
LVHW050555160826
845677LV00011B/2315